QANON

The Truth Behind the Conspiracy
Theory Against United States &
Deep State

2

advice. The content within this book has been derived from various sources. Please consult a licensed professional before attempting any techniques outlined in this book.

By reading this document, the reader agrees that under no circumstances is the author responsible for any losses, direct or indirect, which are incurred as a result of the use of information contained within this document, including, but not limited to, — errors, omissions, or inaccuracies.

TABLE OF CONTENTS

INTRODUCTION

QAnon is a far-right conspiracy theory suggesting that a group of Satan-worshiping pedophiles running a global ring of child sex slavery is conspiring against President Donald Trump. He is fighting them, leading to a "reckoning day" involving journalists and politicians' mass arrests.

While followed by similar viral conspiracies like Pizzagate, the proper theory started with an October 2017 post on the anonymous 4chan imageboard by "Q," who was supposedly an American entity, but most likely become a group of individuals. Q claimed that it had access to sensitive information that concerned the Trump administration and its opponents in the United States. NBC News noticed that the initial Q post was taken by three people and spread over various media outlets to create internet follow-ups for profit. Several related anonymous 4chan posters have preceded QAnon, such as CIAAnon, WH Insider Anon, FBIAnon, and HLIAnon (High-Level Insider).

Q has accused many liberal actors in Hollywood, Democratic leaders, and high-ranking officials of being cartel members. Q also reported that Trump feigned collusion with Russians to recruit Robert Mueller to assist him in revealing the ring and preventing a coup d'etat by Barack Obama, George Soros, and Hillary Clinton. "Q" is a reference to the Q clearance utilized by the United States. Energy Department. QAnon advocates usually tag their social media posts with the hashtag #WG1WGA, which means "Where We Go One, We Go All."

In August 2018, QAnon adherents started appearing at Trump campaign rallies for reelection. A picture opportunity with Trump in the Oval Office in August 2018 was given to T.V. and radio personality Michael "Lionel" Lebron, a proponent of the theory. In July 2019, Bill Mitchell, a broadcaster who supports QAnon, attended a "social media conference" at the White House. A man warming up the audience before Trump spoke at a rally in August 2019 used the QAnon slogan "where we go one, we go everything" and later denied it was a reference to QAnon. This happened hours after a report was released that the FBI had designated QAnon a possible source of domestic terrorism, the first time the agency had so classified a radical conspiracy theory. As of August 2020, Trump had amplified QAnon messaging at least 216 times by retweeting or referencing 129 QAnon-affiliated Twitter accounts, often several times a day, according to an analysis conducted by Media Matters.

By 2020, the number of adherents to QAnon was uncertain, but they had a strong presence on social media, particularly on Twitter. In June 2020, Q, using the Twitter hashtag # TakeTheOath, exhorted followers to take a "digital soldiers oath," and many did. Twitter suspended thousands of QAnon-affiliated accounts in July 2020 and changed their algorithms to reduce the spread of the theory. An internal Facebook study published in August found millions of followers across thousands of groups and pages; later that month, Facebook acted to eliminate and limit QAnon activity. Followers have moved to dedicated boards with messages like EndChan and 8kun, where they coordinated digital warfare to influence the 2020 elections.

In the period of President Donald Trump's term in office, the far-right fringe community known as QAnon has shifted from obscure messages on 4chan message boards to the White

House Press briefing room. On Wednesday, the US. President made his most detailed remarks to date in discussing a cartoon yet mutating conspiracy theory that features him as his crusading savior.

In the period of President Donald Trump's term in office, the far-right fringe culture known as QAnon has advanced from obscure messages on 4chan message boards to the White House Press briefing room — where, on Wednesday, the US. president made his most detailed remarks to date in discussing a cartoon yet mutating conspiracy theory that portrays him as his crusading savior.

Trump's comments were ambiguous, so it's unclear how tuned he is to the full spectrum of QAnon's worldview. He addressed the theory's broad outlines and its perceived position.

"Alright, I don't know much about the campaign, but I understand they like me —

which I appreciate," he said. He said, "I heard these people love our country."

A reporter asked him directly about "this idea that you secretly rescue the world from this satanic cult of pedophiles and cannibals. Does it sound like something behind you or a believer?"

"OK, I haven't heard," Trump responded. "Why is that meant to be a bad thing or a good thing? I mean, you know, if I can help save the planet from problems, I'm happy to do it.

Trump tweeted last week's congratulations to a Georgian Republican congressional primary winner who has supported QAnon theories in the past and could be going to Congress next year but refused on Friday to answer QAnon questions reporter.

Fellow Republicans weighed quickly. "Why wouldn't the president knock Q'anon's butts in the world? Nut jobs, racists [sic], haters have no room in either group," tweeted former Florida gov. Jeb Bush.

Chapter 1: QANON: WHAT IS IT AND WHERE DID IT COME FROM?

President Trump talked about how followers of QAnon's conspiracy theory, which has evolved online in the US., seem to like him a lot.

Mr. Trump told journalists he didn't know anything about the campaign but added that "there were people who love our country."

Facebook and Twitter face a backlash that has taken action against thousands of accounts and web addresses linked to videos and blogs sharing QAnon's strange ideas.

Then what's QAnon, and who believes?

What's it?

At the core, QAnon is a large, baseless conspiracy theory that claims President Trump is waging a secret war against elite Satan-worshiping pedophiles in government, industry, and media.

QAnon believers have predicted that this battle would lead to a day of reckoning to arrest and execute famous people, including former presidential candidate Hillary Clinton.

That's the basic tale, but there are so many offshoots, detours, and internal disputes that QAnon's total list of arguments is huge — and sometimes contradictory. Adherents draw their own far-fetched conclusions in reporting, historical evidence, and numerology.

Where began it all?

An anonymous user posted 4chan on the message board in October 2017. The user signed off as "Q," citing a US. security approval standard known as "Q clearance."

These messages became known as "Q drops" or "breadcrumbs," sometimes written with slogans, promises, and pro-Trump themes in cryptic language.

Nobody believes, right?

It's thousands. Since 2017, the amount of traffic to popular social networking sites such as Facebook, Twitter, Reddit, and YouTube has exploded, suggesting that numbers have risen further during the coronavirus pandemic.

Social media judging, hundreds of thousands of people believe in some of QAnon's weird theories.

And its success wasn't affected by incidents that seemed to contradict the whole thing. For example, early Q drops focused on prosecutor Robert Mueller's investigation.

QAnon supporters believed Mr. Mueller's inquiry into Russian involvement in the 2016 US. election was just an elaborate cover story for pedophile investigation. As it ended with no such bombshell announcement, conspiracy theorists' focus slipped elsewhere.

True believers argue that intentional disinformation is sown in Q's messages, rendering the conspiracy theory challenging to disprove.

What was the impact?

QAnon supporters push hashtags and organize harassment of alleged enemies — pedophiles' officials, celebrities, and journalists they claim are a cover-up.

Not all abusive posts online. Twitter says it took action against QAnon due to possible "offline damage."

Several QAnon believers were arrested following threats or offline intervention.

In a notable case in 2018, a heavily armed man blocked the Hoover Dam bridge. Matthew Wright later pled guilty to charges of terrorism.

Will it influence U.S. election?

Studies suggest most Americans haven't experienced QAnon. But for many believers, it is the cornerstone of President Trump's popularity.

Mr. Trump had replaced QAnon backers, knowingly or not, and his son Eric Trump shared a QAnon meme on Instagram last month.

Dozens of QAnon backers run for November's Congress. Many have little hope, but some, including Georgia's Marjorie Taylor Greene, seems to have a strong chance of winning a place.

Chapter 2: THE ORIGIN AND HISTORY OF CONSPIRACY THEORIES

ONJAN. ONJAN. 30,1835, when Andrew Jackson left the congressman's funeral, the assassin drew a pistol and pointed it to the president. The gun misfired. The gunman pulled another weapon. Although loaded, the fire failed too. The cane-wielding Jackson and several witnesses overpowered the would-be killer, named Richard Lawrence. Lawrence later told interrogators he was King Richard III, and Jackson killed his father. He was insane and sent to an asylum. Lawrence was lonely.

Or at least the official story. It wasn't long before two witnesses filed affidavits saying they saw Lawrence at Mississippi Sen's home shortly before the attack. Poindexter was a Jackson administration foe, and pro-Jackson newspapers accused the senator of planning the president's murder.

Some of Jackson's opponents responded by claiming that the president had engineered the attack to gain public support, justifying why both guns failed. And many

Jacksonians fingered at South Carolina's Sen. John Calhoun.

When Republican writer John Smith Dye described the crime 29 years later, he saw a more devilish plot at work. Calhoun may not have been directly involved, Dye admitted. But Dye believed Calhoun was part of a greater force, the Slave Power, that would have gained if Jackson were placed on the field. And he was informed that the Slave Force had killed two more U.S. presidents — William Henry Harrison and Zachary Taylor — and that another, James Buchanan, narrowly avoided death at their hands.

Assassination theorists weren't the only Americans concerned about slaveholders' conspiracies. Dye did not coin the word "Slave Force." The term was popular usage in the North, used to describe the planter elite's political influence. This was not a conspiracy theory in itself, but it also followed conspiracy paintings. According to historian Russel B. Nye, the Slave Power had an alleged goal to spread slavery "to territories and free states (possibly whites)" and "to abolish civil rights, regulate federal government policy, and complete the establishment of a national ruling class based on slave agriculture."

Meanwhile, Southerners had their intricate conspiracy theories, blaming actual and imaginary slave revolts on the machinations of rebellion-facing abolitionists, dangerous land pirates, and other outside agitators.

It's been a tense moment. In America, it's still suspicious.

THE FEAR OF conspiracies was a dominant force across the political spectrum, from the Colonial period to the present, both in the mainstream and at the extremes. Conspiracy theories played significant roles in conflicts from 17th-century Indian wars to Gilded Age labor struggles, from the American Revolution to the War on Terror.

Unfortunately, much of the public understanding of political paranoia appears to be stuck in 1964, when historian Richard Hofstadter published "The Paranoid Style of American Politics." Hofstadter set out to describe a "shape of mind" characterized by "heated hysteria, skepticism, and conspiratorial imagination," finding it in movements ranging from the anti-Masonic and anti-Catholic crusades of the 19th century.

The essay has some important observations, and if nothing else, can remind readers that conspiracy theories are not an innovation. But it also notes that political paranoia is "just a minority type."

Hofstadter didn't have statistics to support that inference. However, we have some data on the prevalence of well-known conspiracy theories, and findings do not support his sweeping argument. A national survey in 2006 suggested that 36 percent of the people polled — a minority but not a moderate one — believed it to be "extremely" or "somewhat" possible that U.S. politicians either allowed 9/11 to happen or actively orchestrated the attacks. Theories about JFK's assassination aren't a minority taste at all: Forty years after John F. Kennedy was shot, an ABC News poll found 70 % of the country believing a conspiracy was behind the death of the president.

Skilled progressives also have conspiracy theories. By that, I don't mean establishment members often accept a disreputable theory — although that happens. Often the center supports theories that are no less cynical than the fringe's opinions.

Remember the "political outrage" phenomenon, where fear and hysteria are magnified, distorted, and maybe even generated by powerful social institutions. The sociologist Stanley Cohen sketched the traditional progression of a moral panic in 1972: "An event, episode, individual or group of people emerges to be described as a danger to societal values and interests; its existence is portrayed by mass media in a stylized and stereotypical fashion; moral barricades are staffed by editors, priests, politicians, and other right-thinking people;

A moral panic's essential feature is a folk devil — typically a scapegoat who is not liable for the danger. The folk devil also takes the form of a conspiracy: a Satanic cult, a strong gang, militia backwoods. Cohen's case study is British, but American equivalents. One is the early 20th-century anti-prostitution hysteria, featuring lurid tales of a massive multinational white-slavery syndicate conscripting thousands of young girls into sexual service each year. A former Chicago prosecutor said the syndicate was "invisible government," "hidden hand," and "secret force."

Coerced prostitution still existed, but it wasn't as widespread or structured as implied the wild rhetoric. And far from being consigned to a small minority campaign, the scare led to a significant piece of national legislation, the 1910 Mann Act, giving the organization the first big boost that would later be known as the FBI. Within a decade, the office will broaden its purview from alleged pimp conspiracies to alleged communist conspiracies, receiving another boost throughout the process.

The consequence was a warped image in which fear consumes the world's outsiders, and its establishment is generally not. The essay had space for "Greenback and Populist writers who created a great conspiracy of multinational bankers." Still, it said little about the intellectuals of the period who viewed Populism as a conspiracy.

While academics and analysts do not believe hysteria is limited to political extremes, they often say it results from, especially harsh times. In 2009, conservative writer David Frum gave the reason for Glenn Beck's fame, a rightwing broadcaster with conspiracy stories fondness. "Conspiracy theories," Frum wrote, "flourish in economic downturns."

They thrive during economic downturns. But they still excel during economic upturns. For his involvement in the possibility that the Federal Emergency Management Agency was constructing underground detention camps, Frum criticized Beck. Hence, it's worth remembering that the same paranoia was common on the left during the booming 80s and on the right during the booming 90s. For the last few decades, members of every party out of control have worried that the power party will become authoritarian. (Beck finally rejected FEMA story.)

Even if you put aside strictly political fears, the 1990s, a period of relative peace and prosperity, were also a golden age of plainly fictitious, supposedly real, conspiracy stories. There are many explanations for this, including the fact that the U.S. is riven by wars even at its most stable. But there's also the risk that peace will lift fears as easily as war. Anthropologist David Graeber concluded that "it's the most peaceful communities that are often the most plagued, in their inventive conceptions of the universe, by relentless specters of perpetual warfare." Venezuela's Piaroa Indians, he wrote, "are popular for their peacefulness," yet "they inhabit a world of endless invisible warfare in which wizards are engaged in battling I's attacks.

ONNOCT. The CBS radio network transmitted "The Battle of the Worlds" 30,1938. Orson Welles' broadcast, directed and narrated, was based on H. G. Wells' popular novel about Earth's Martian invasion, but the action shifted from Victorian England to New Jersey. It was and is a brilliant and powerful film, but today's broadcast is recognized for reasons far beyond its creative standard.

You will think you know this story. In common memory, listener crowds mistook the play for a real alien invasion, setting off mass hysteria. The reality was boring but fascinating. There were also listeners who, obviously ignoring the initial announcement that the story was fiction, took the show at face value and thought there was a true invasion going on. But they don't seem to be more popular than people today who confuse satires for actual newspaper stories in The Onion. Mass hysteria was imaginary.

After the play aired, influential political analyst Walter Lippmann took the opportunity to warn about "crowds that drift with all the winds that blow and are eventually caught in the great hurricanes," adding that those "masses without roots" and their "volcanic and violent energy" are "the turmoil in which the new Caesars are born."

"Capture consciousness": what a chilling image. This idea emerges when critics claim that our leaders use mass media to brainwash us. But you can also find concern in those leaders themselves, who have a long history of worrying about any new means of communication. If Orson Welles was cast as a magician with the power to cloud men's minds, his listeners were easily exploited as a senseless mob.

The story of "Battle of the Worlds" is generally told as a parable of mainstream hysteria — a sudden increase in the kind of fear that Hofstadter's essay decried. But at least as much, it's a parable about bourgeois hysteria — the anti-populist paranoia exemplified by Hofstadter's essay. No history of American paranoia can be complete except for the latter.

Chapter 3: QANON EXPLAINED: THE ANTISEMITIC CONSPIRACY THEORY GAINING TRACTION AROUND THE WORLD

To Donald Trump, "people love our country." It's a possible domestic terror threat to the FBI. And for you or someone else who has signed on to Facebook in recent months, it might just be a friend or family member who has started to show a disturbing interest in child trafficking, the "cabal," or conspiracy theories concerning Bill Gates and the coronavirus.

This is QAnon, an Internet conspiracy theory that entered the American mainstream in August. For years, the movement has festered on the fringes of rightwing internet communities, but its popularity has exploded in recent months amid the coronavirus pandemic's social turmoil and confusion.

"QAnon" is an unfounded internet conspiracy theory whose adherents claim that a group of Satan-worshipping

Democrats, Hollywood celebrities, and billionaires rules the planet while engaging in pedophilia, sex trafficking, and extracting from the blood of abused children an allegedly life-extending chemist. QAnon followers believe Donald Trump is waging a covert war against this conspiracy and its "deep-state" allies to uncover the malefactors and send them back to Guantánamo.

There are many, many QAnon story threads, many as far-fetched and evidence-free as the rest, including subplots, focused on living John F Kennedy Jr (he isn't), the Rothschild family controlling many banks (they don't), and children being sold through the furniture retailer Wayfair website (they aren't). Hillary Clinton, Barack Obama, George Soros, Bill Gates, Tom Hanks, Oprah Winfrey, Chrissy Teigen, and Pope Francis are just some of the celebrities QAnon followers cast in their alternate universe as villains.

This sounds familiar. Haven't we seen this before?

Yeah, yeah. QAnon has its origins in conspiracy theories, some relatively modern, others a millennium old.

The current antecedent is Pizzagate, the conspiracy theory that went viral during the 2016 presidential campaign when rightwing news outlets and influencers spread the groundless notion that food references and famous Washington DC pizza restaurant in Clinton campaign manager John Podesta's stolen emails were possibly a secret code for a child trafficking ring. The hypothesis touched on the restaurant and its employees' extreme abuse, resulting in a December 2016 shooting by a man who had traveled to the restaurant, thinking there were children in need of rescue.

QAnon emerged from Pizzagate and contained much of the same basic characters and plotlines without the irrefutable details. Yet QAnon has its origins in far older conspiracy theories. The notion of the all-powerful, world-ruling conspiracy derives directly from the Protocols of the Elders of Zion, a false document aimed at revealing a Jewish plot to rule the world used in the 20th century to justify antisemitism. Another QAnon canard — the theory that cabal members harvest the chemical adrenochrome from their child victims' blood and eat it to prolong their lives — is a new reversal of age-old antisemitic blood libel.

How started QAnon?

On October 28th, 2017, "Q" emerged from the Internet's primordial swamp on the 4chan message board with a post confidently stating that Hillary Clinton's "extradition" was "already in motion" and her imminent arrest. In subsequent posts – so far more than 4,000 – Q built his legacy as a government insider with top security clearance who knew the truth about Trump's covert power struggle with the "deep state."

When posting anonymously, Q uses a "tripcode" to differentiate its posts from those of other anonymous users (known as "anons"). Q moved from posting on 4chan to posting on 8chan in November 2017, silenced several months after 8chan shut down in August 2019, and finally re-emerged on a new website set up by 8chan 's owner, 8kun.

Q's posts are enigmatic, elliptic. They also consist of a long string of leading questions intended to direct readers to discover the "truth" through "testing" As with the supposed "extradition" of Clinton, Q has repeatedly made predictions that have disappointed. Still, true believers prefer to change their narratives to account for inconsistencies.

For near QAnon followers, the posts (or "drops") contain knowledge "crumbs" they "bake" into "proofs." For "bakers," QAnon is both a fun hobby and a critical call. It's a kind of participatory internet scavenger hunt with extraordinarily high stakes and fellow adherents' ready-made culture.

How do you go from 4chan anonymous messages to full conspiracy?

Not by mistake, certainly. Anonymous internet posters pretending to have access to classified information are fairly popular and typically vanish once people lose interest or realize they're tricked. (Liberal variations of this phenomenon were widespread in the early months of Trump administration when hundreds of Twitter accounts claiming to be operated by federal agency employees went viral.)

QAnon may have died away, if not for the committed work of three conspiracy theorists who at the very beginning latched on it and converted it into a digestible narrative for popular social media networks. A 2018 NBC News investigation revealed how this trio worked together to spread and benefit from QAnon, turning it into today's massive, multi-platform internet phenomenon. There is now a whole QAnon media ecosystem, with vast quantities of video material, memes, e-books, chatrooms, and more, all designed to snare potential recruits' attention, then pull them "down the rabbit hole" into QAnon's alternative truth.

How many people trust QAnon? Who are they?

Nobody knows, but it's safe to presume at least 100,000 people.

Conspiracy experts point out that QAnon's conviction is far from popular. Although at one point 80 % of Americans believed a conspiracy theory about the Kennedy assassination, a March poll by Pew Research showed that 76% of Americans had never heard of QAnon, and only 3% knew "a lot" about it.

QAnon's biggest Facebook groups had around 200,000 participants in them until Facebook suspended them mid-August. When Twitter took similar action in July against QAnon accounts, it restricted functionality for around 150,000 users. In June, a Q drop containing a connection to a year-old Guardian article resulted in around 150,000 views over the next 24 hours.

These are rough figures to conclude from, but they suggest online activity size in the absence of better statistics.

Overall, QAnon seems most common among older Republicans and evangelical Christians. QAnon subcultures exist for people pursuing learning Q drops like Bible study. Most adherents seem to have come to QAnon from New Age spiritual movements, more conventional conspiracy theory groups, or far right. Because Trump adulation is a prerequisite, it is almost exclusively a conservative movement, while # SaveTheChildren 's campaign helps make inroads among non-Trump supporters (see below).

QAnon spread to Latin America and Europe, where some far-right groups seem to catch on.

Why is QAnon important?

Second, there's violence in danger. Those who genuinely believe that influential figures keep kids hostage to manipulate them sexually or for their blood, taking action to stop violence can seem like a moral imperative. Although most QAnon adherents would not participate in violence, many have already or have tried, so the FBI classified the movement as a possible domestic terror threat. Participation in QAnon most sometimes entails aggressive online abuse campaigns against suspected rivals, which can adversely harm the targets.

QAnon is also gaining momentum as a Republican party political power, which could have immediate, detrimental effects on American democracy. Media Matters assembled a list of 77 congressional seat candidates who expressed support for QAnon, and at least one of them, Georgia's Marjorie Taylor Greene, is expected to be elected in November.

Trump, as the ultimate story hero, has the unique potential to influence QAnon believers. On August 19, a White House press conference gave him the chance to dismiss the hypothesis once and for all. Instead, he praised the adherents of QAnon as patriots and seemed to affirm the core principle of belief, saying: "If I can help save the world from problems, I'm willing to do it; I'm willing to put myself out there, and we are, in reality. We're saving the world from a far-left ideology that would kill this country and imitate the rest of the world when this country is gone.

Faithful QAnon rejoiced.

Didn't you # SaveTheChildren? What's that about?

Participating in QAnon consists primarily of "research"—i.e., learning more about Byzantine theories or decoding Q drops — and evangelism. Most proselytization relies on media manipulation techniques designed to capture users' attention and send them to a regulated online media environment where they are "red-pilled" by consuming pro-QAnon content.

For years, QAnon adherents have used various online strategies to gain virality and mass media attention, including making "documentaries" full of disinformation, hijacking trending hashtags with QAnon messages, appearing at Trump rallies with Q flags, or running for public office.

This summer, a very strong version of this strategy emerged with the #SaveTheChildren or #SaveOurChildren initiative. The harmless sounding hashtag, historically used by anti-child trafficking NGOs, has been overwhelmed by QAnon adherents hinting at the wider QAnon narrative. (It doesn't help that sex trafficking is still full of false statistics.)

On Facebook, child hysteria due to the coronavirus pandemic, a resurgent anti-vaxx campaign, and QAnon-fuelled sex trafficking scaremongering have all combined to trigger a modern-day moral panic, much like the 1980s "Satanic Panic."

Hundreds of real-life "Save Our Children" demonstrations have been organized on Facebook in the U.S. (and worldwide) communities. These small protests, in turn, push local news coverage by outlets that don't know that by reporting news designed to "raise awareness" about child trafficking, they inspire their readers or viewers to go online, where a search for "save our kids" might lead them straight down the QAnon rabbit hole.

Chapter 4: THE PSYCHOLOGY OF CONSPIRACY THEORIES

What psychological factors drive conspiracy theories' popularity, explaining important events as secret plots by powerful and evil groups? What are the psychological consequences of these theories? We review the current research and find it responds more thoroughly than the first of these questions. Belief in conspiracy theories seems to be driven by motives that can be characterized as epistemic (understanding one's environment), existential (being safe and controlling one's environment), and social (keeping a positive self-image and social group). Little research has investigated the consequences of conspiracy belief, and so far, this research has not shown that conspiracy belief fulfills people's motivations. Instead, for many, conspiracy beliefs may be more appealing than satisfying. Further research is needed to determine whom conspiracy theories can meet key psychological motives and under what conditions.

Over a third of Americans believe that global warming is a hoax (Swift, 2013), and over half believe that Lee Harvey Oswald was not alone in John F. Kennedy's assassination (Jensen, 2013). Examples of conspiracy theories — explanations of important events involving secret plots by powerful and malevolent groups (e.g., Goertzel, 1994). In recent years there has been developing interest in the psychological factors that drive conspiracy theories' popularity. In this book, we draw together and organize findings from this research. This research propose that people may be drawn to conspiracy theories when compared to non-conspiracy explanations; they promise to satisfy important social-psychological motives that can be characterized as epistemic (for instance, the desire for understanding, subjective certainty, and accuracy), existential (e.g., the desire for security and control), and social (e.g., the desire to maintain a positive). This taxonomy, derived from system-justification theory, serves as a useful heuristic to classify conspiracy-related motives. The comparatively scarce research examining the consequences of conspiracy theories, however, does not indicate that they ultimately help people fulfill these motives.

Epistemic Motives

Seeking causal explanations for events is central to building a stable, reliable, and internally consistent world understanding (Heider, 1958). Relevant epistemic motives that may serve causal explanations involve slaking curiosity when knowledge is unavailable, that uncertainty and confusion when available information clashes, finding meaning when occurrences seem unpredictable, and defending beliefs from disconfirmation. Related to these reasons, conspiracy theories have characteristics that differentiate them from other causal explanations. Although they are theoretical to varying degrees, they postulate acts that are hidden from public scrutiny, complex in that they postulate the coordination of multiple actors, and immune to falsification in that they postulate that conspirators use deception and misinformation to cover up their actions — implying that people who try to refute conspiracy theories – themselves be part of them.

A related property of conspiracy theories is that they can defend cherished beliefs (e.g., vaccination is harmful; climate change is not a serious concern) by presenting predominantly dis-confirmatory facts (e.g., scientific findings) as the result of a conspiracy (Lewandowsky, Oberauer, & Gignac, 2013).

In general, empirically-based (vs. speculative), parsimonious (vs. complex), and falsifiable explanations are stronger by normative causal explanation standards (e.g., in science; see Grimes, 2016). However, conspiracy theories seem to provide broad, internally consistent explanations that enable people to maintain convictions against confusion and inconsistency. Research suggests that conspiracy theories' confidence is higher when the desire to find patterns in the world is experimentally increased (Whitson & Galinsky, 2008). It is also stronger among people habitually seeking environmental significance and patterns, including believers in paranormal phenomena (e.g., Bruder, Haffke, Neave, Nouripanah, & Imhoff, 2013; but see Dieguez, Wagner-Egger, & Gauvrit, 2015). It also tends to be stronger when incidents are particularly large or important, leaving people frustrated with boring, small-scale explanations (Leman & Cinnirella, 2013). Moreover, the need for cognitive closure is related to beliefs in relevant conspiracy theories for incidents lacking simple official explanations (Marchlewska, Cichocka, & Kossowska, 2017). Research also suggests conspiracy conviction is greater when people experience anxiety from feeling unsure (van Prooijen & Jostmann, 2013).

Our analysis suggests that conspiracy theories can fulfill certain epistemic interests at others' cost — such as protecting beliefs from ambiguity while less likely to be true. The epistemic limitations of conspiracy theories do not seem readily apparent to people lacking the ability or incentive to think critically and rationally. Conspiracy theories are correlated with lower critical thinking levels (Swami, Voracek, Stieger, Tran, & Furnham, 2014) and lower education levels (Douglas, Sutton, Callan, Dawtry, & Harvey, 2016). It is also related to the tendency to overestimate the probability of co-occurring events (Brotherton & French, 2014) and the tendency to interpret agency and intentionality where there is no such thing (Douglas et al., 2016).

Given their objective or normative limits, how well do conspiracy theories fulfill the epistemic motivations attracting people? Relatively little research has addressed this topic, indicating they may be more appealing than satisfying. Extreme and ingrained attitude attitudes, on the one hand, are correlated with conspiracy theories, indicating that they can help people protect theories from disconfirmation (Uscinski, Klofstad, & Atkinson, 2016). Recent studies, however, suggest that making compelling arguments for conspiracy theories about vaccines (Jolley & Douglas, 2014a) and climate change (Jolley & Douglas, 2014b) raises their uncertainty levels.

Existential Motives

As well as their purely epistemic purposes, causal explanations serve people's need to feel safe and secure in their environment and to exercise control over the environment as autonomous individuals and collectives (Tetlock, 2002). Several early conspiracy theories suggested that people turn to conspiracy theories for compensatory gratification when challenged. For instance, people who lack instrumental control may get some compensatory sense of control through conspiracy theories because they offer them the opportunity to reject official narratives and feel they have an alternative account

(Goertzel, 1994). Conspiracy theories can promise to make people feel safer as a method of cheater detection, identifying dangerous and untrustworthy individuals, and reducing or neutralizing their threat (Bost & Prunier, 2013).

Research supports this account of conspiracy theory motivation. Studies have shown that people can turn to conspiracy theories when nervous (Grzesiak-Feldman, 2013) and feel powerless (Abalakina-Paap, Stephan, Craig, & Gregory, 1999). Other research shows that conspiracy theories are strongly linked to a lack of socio-political influence or psychological empowerment (Bruder et al., 2013). Experiments have shown that conspiracy belief is heightened when people feel unable to influence events when their sense of control is reinforced (van Prooijen & Acker, 2015).

Unfortunately, research so far has not shown that conspiracy belief effectively satisfies this motivation. Instead, experimental exposure to conspiracy theories tends to rapidly undermine people's sense of autonomy and control (Douglas and Leite, 2017; Jolley and Douglas, 2014a, 2014b). These studies have also shown that it makes people less inclined to take action to improve their autonomy and control in the long run. Specifically, they are less inclined to engage with their organizations and mainstream political processes such as voting and party politics. In addition, exposure to conspiracy theories may otherwise implicitly undermine people's autonomy. Douglas and Sutton (2008) showed that people were successfully convinced by pro-conspiracy information but were unaware of being persuaded. They wrongly believed that their pre-exposure conviction was similar to their new beliefs. Because conspiracy theories suggest that important results are in the hands of malevolent forces possessing and exercising powers beyond legitimate limits, it would not be surprising if further research suggests that their effect is often disempowering.

Social Motives

Causal explanations, including conspiracy explanations, are often influenced by different social motivations, including the desire to participate and maintain a good self-image and in-group. Scholars also indicated that conspiracy theories favor self and in-group by having others to blame for negative outcomes. Thus, they can help to maintain the self-image and the in-group as competent and moral but sabotaged by powerful and unscrupulous others. If so, we should expect conspiracy theories to be especially appealing to people who find their self or positive in-group image threatened (Cichocka, Marchlewska, & Golec de Zavala, 2016).

The study typically supports this expectation. Experimental results suggest that ostracism experiences cause people to believe in superstitions and conspiracy theories, apparently in an effort to make sense of their experience (Graeupner & Coman, 2017). Members of groups whose ethnicity (Crocker, Luhtanen, Broadnax, & Blaine, 1999) or income is objectively low (vs. high) are more likely to endorse conspiracy theories. People on the losing side of political processes often seem more inclined to believe conspiracy theories (Uscinski & Parent, 2014). Conspiracy belief was also related to discrimination against influential groups (Imhoff & Bruder, 2014) and enemies (Kofta & Sedek, 2005).

These results indicate that conspiracy theories may be employed defensively to alleviate the self or in-group sense of guilt for their disadvantaged position. Consistent with this defensive motivation, conspiracy belief is associated with narcissism—a self-inflated view that requires external validation and is linked to paranoid ideation (Cichocka, Marchlewska, & Golec de Zavala, 2016). Collective narcissism also predicts conspiracy belief—a belief in the in-group's greatness coupled with a belief that other people do not appreciate it enough (Cichocka, Marchlewska, Golec de Zavala, & Olechowski, 2016). Groups feeling oppressed are more likely to support conspiracy theories about influential out-groups (Bilewicz, Winiewski, Kofta, & Wójcik, 2013).

While people are strongly drawn to conspiracy theories when their social motives are frustrated, following these theories is not at all simple as a successful way to satisfy these motivations. A feature of conspiracy theories is their negative, distrustful representation of others. Thus, it is possible that they are not only a symptom but also a source of the feelings of alienation and anomie — a feeling of personal dissatisfaction and lack of social world understanding — with which they are associated (e.g., Abalakina-Paap et al., 1999). Experiments show that exposure to conspiracy theories reduces confidence in government institutions, while conspiracy theories are unrelated to those institutions (Einstein & Glick, 2015). It also disappoints politicians and scientists (Jolley & Douglas, 2014a). Therefore, empirical research suggests that conspiracy theories serve to erode social capital and may frustrate the need for people to see themselves as valuable members of morally decent collectives.

Summary, Caveats, and Future Research

Research has thus far successfully articulated some of the motives that, together with deficiencies in available knowledge, cognitive capacity, and critical thinking motivation, can contribute to conspiracy belief. Although researchers have theorized about the impact of conspiracy theories on their followers and culture, very little empirical study has been undertaken to investigate them. Nevertheless, preliminary work indicates that despite the allure of conspiracy theories for people who have epistemic, psychological, and social motivations, they could eventually further thwart those motivations. In this context, conspiracy theories can be considered an ironic or self-defeating form of motivated social cognition. There is reason to expect further research to corroborate this preliminary picture because, as we have shown, conspiracy theories have certain characteristics that do not enable themselves to satisfy these motives — for example, they are typically unfounded and contradictory, they portray the public as naive and at the hands of unaccountable forces, and they impute highly antisocial and cynical motives.

Nonetheless, there is reason to expect future studies to show that conspiracy theories meet certain people's needs. Hitherto, the longitudinal research performed has identified communities (undergraduate students and survey panelists) that are not especially vulnerable or endangered and typically do not support conspiracy theories. These people would undoubtedly view conspiracy theories as disturbing, destabilizing, and potentially alienating. However, these people aren't what scholars had in mind when they argued that occasionally conspiracy theories might be adaptive. They involve groups and individuals alienated from society and for whom conspiracy theories can provide some compensation. These involve disempowered groups that can use conspiracy theories to subvert hierarchies of authority by formulating their interpretation of fact (Sapountzis & Condor, 2013) and promoting unity and collective action (Adams, O'Brien & Nelson, 2006). In these cultures, and even in online communities where conspiracy theories reflect normative or even official positions (e.g., 9/11 Truth movement), belief in a conspiracy may provide an important source of identity and shared fact. Moreover, history has consistently shown business, and political leaders conspire against public interests. Conspiracy theories play an important role in exposing their misdeeds.

Regulated longitudinal and experimental studies of vulnerable and endangered communities must perform fair tests of conspiracy theory utility. Specifically, future research needs to investigate individuals whose psychological needs are clinically or experimentally compromised, to assess if conspiracy theories bring them closer or further away from meeting these needs. In one concept, Jolley, Douglas, and Sutton (2017) exposed people to challenges to their social system's legitimacy. They found the harmful impact of these attacks on status quo satisfaction was removed when participants were also exposed to conspiracy theories. Therefore, conspiracy theories tended to shield people from the impact of attacks on the status quo.

We reviewed existing literature on psychological factors that seem to influence conspiracy beliefs. We conclude that conspiracy theories seem to derive primarily from epistemic, psychological, and social motivations. Research has yet to prove it serves these purposes efficiently, and early signs are that it can sometimes thwart them. Therefore, conspiracy belief is a self-defeating type of motivated social cognition. However, important issues remain open. More regulated research is required on the effects of conspiracy theories, particularly on marginalized and disadvantaged groups defined as most likely to benefit from them. We hope this analysis will act as an organizing scheme for potential conspiracy psychology studies.

Chapter 5: QANON IS HERE TO STAY. IS IT THE FUTURE OF OUR POLITICS?

Some anti-lockdown mob won't even know what QAnon is, but will still recite their talk points. A conspiracy worldwide. Satanic elite fear. The planet about a 'great awakening.'

On August 29, the crazies may well be out. Despite a police crackdown and several pre-emptive arrests, a loose coalition of lockdown opponents and COVID-19 truthers are set to rally around the country to mark "freedom day."

Some say COVID-19 is a hoax, no worse than flu. Others worry about 5 G towers. There will be plenty of anti-vaxxers and crunchy forms of Byron Bay New Generation. And some will think U.S. President Donald Trump is a messiah battling to free the world from a Satanic conspiracy of pedophiles and child sex traffickers.

What started with an anonymous internet poster alleging a top-level U.S. government "Q Clearance" dropping mysterious breadcrumbs on 4Chan has mushroomed into a common conspiracy theory and millennial doomsday cult. It's classified as a potential FBI domestic terror threat. His supporters committed murder.

In QAnon's world, the satanic conspiracy includes everyone from Hillary Clinton to Ellen DeGeneres and Daniel Andrews. They're selling and drinking their blood. Accelerated by social media, QAnon spread worldwide. It's become a kind of mothership, the conspiracy theory of "big tent," to which all others belong.

Spend time around some of the anti-lockdown demonstrations sputtering around the country since March, and don't skip the QAnon talk points. See # SaveChildren? It's QAnon. Any pedophiles? QAnon. QAnon. "Big Awakening?" Even Q. Six months ago, most Australians will never learn of QAnon outside the extreme internet. Now it's the bond connecting a vast network of anti-lockdown conspiracies.

And, due to the pandemic, it might well have broken into our politics.

Australian-accented QAnon

Just before the pandemic, QAnon steadily closed in just beyond the political fringes. One of Scott Morrison's oldest family members, as Crikey revealed last year, is a Q-believer. An independent candidate with QAnon-influenced social media background ran unsuccessfully at the recent Eden-Monaro byelection.

It began to draw in anti-vaxxers, and conspiracy theorists — most notably NRL WAG turned anti-vax influencer Taylor Winterstein and Pete Evans, the popular chef. But it's the pandemic that made it the mothership.

"Look at every Facebook conspiracy theorist, and you'll see almost unanimously that they've been 'Q-pilled' since March," University of Tasmania professor and online misinformation researcher Kaz Ross tells Crikey.

Some of the anti-lockdown mob won't even know what QAnon is, but will always recite its talk points — a global conspiracy, fear of paedophilic, satanic powers, the "great awakening" nation.

How did QAnon rapidly conquer Australia's conspiracy theory landscape? First, Ross says, like biblical Christianity, QAnon seeks to give meaning and continuity during an apocalyptic moment.

"We know faith is turning and trying to make sense of distressing events. We've been through the horrendous bushfires, so we have the pandemic behind. It's all religious.

QAnon has a strong correlation with centuries-old anti-Semitic conspiracies like blood libel, which the alt-right has actively forced out of internet sewers in recent years.

And finally, there are the anti-vaxxer health groups, highly literate on Instagram, and excellent at spreading junk science across social media. When they started speaking QAnon 's language, those verbal queues — references to the "Great Awakening" and a "gathering storm" penetrated the anti-lockdown lexicon.

What's fascinating is how QAnon flourished in Australia in the absence of a charismatic Trump-like figure, bringing in hippy kinds that would once have been on the political left.

But outside the core values, the great strength of QAnon is its ability to easily subsume other types of conspiratorial thought, pick on new meanings, and develop a distinctly local flavor. QAnon seamlessly integrated 5 G fears and pandemic vaccines.

Online disinformation researcher at Concordia University, Marc-Andre Argentino, described Australia as one of QAnon's "five eyes"—it has one of the world's largest follow-ups.

Regarding Australian QAnon posts in January, Argentino pointed to a peculiar Australian emphasis on bushfires and the Catholic Church.

Politicians targeted

Three years after QAnon began showing up in August, reporters eventually questioned Trump. The president nudged and winked, condemning QAnon. Who was he to disavow people "love our country" and "like me," Trump said.

Marjorie Taylor Greene, a pro-QAnon businesswoman, secured primary GOP in August for a secure Florida congressional seat. Trump named a potential Republican star. Coming November, Congress will have many QAnon-supporters.

In Australia, QAnon has been coming out of the political shadows in recent months. Last week, Nationals MP Anne Webster fought a defamation fight against Karen Brewer, a conspiracy theorist who had accused her of being part of a pedophile network.

As Victoria's crossbench prepared to vote this week to expand the state's emergency laws, hundreds of M.P.s were bombarded with threatening messages, mostly from QAnon backers, after exchanging their phone numbers in anti-lockdown groups.

Dan Andrews is now QAnon Australia's number one public enemy, Ross says. He's accused of being a pedophile. Believers also appeared at his election office, and he's one of the politicians copping a torrent of threats.

Politics' Future?

Australia's politics have always been a bit more serious than America's. It's harder for

Q-infused crazies to leap from fringes to mainstream politics. But QAnon believers needn't be in parliament to affect our elections for the worse.

The death tax scare was a mostly forgotten footnote to Labor's 2019 election choke, a Facebook propaganda effort with little foundation in the party platform. Labor candidates felt the ground moving under them, fighting an unlikely battle against a viral myth that wouldn't go anywhere.

Since 2016, delicate, normie technocrats like Bill Shorten have struggled to find a response to fake turbo-charged politics. All QAnon followers need to do is clutter newsfeeds with enough white noise, and a close election could start shifting. If Facebook threatens to block news content in Australia, it might become even easier.

In the U.S., and to some degree in Australia, right-wing misinformation kills rivalry in Facebook's eyeballs war. The Trump team knows these very fine people, radicalized by Facebook, are key to his chances of re-election.

It's not unplausible that an Australian candidate might really start tapping into the disinformation, winking at a rising chorus of revived Q-believers.

And whatever happens to Trump in November, those believers will rise. Since Q provides no daily existence. It's a wonderful story. It has heroes, villains. It helps people make sense of a strange, incomprehensible, and sometimes grim world. It's no surprise that Adrienne LaFrance of The Atlantic, in one of QAnon 's landmark writings, calls it a new American religion.

When QAnon rabbit hole adherents collapse, they are always so feverishly pulled into the parallel universe that they let their offline relationships wither and die. Q offers the reason and hopes they need. They are patriots, citizen journalists, internet sleuths gathering bits of a great, terrible truth, helping to save the world from a terrible evil.

Mainstream politics, media, organizations intended to give people hope, sense, clarification and comfort have failed to do so. Their argument is far less convincing. And as long as that's real, QAnon will remain here.

WANT TO UNDERSTAND AMERICAN POLITICS?

April 15, 2013 — Twin bomb explosions explode near the Boston Marathon end, killing three and injuring at least 264. One suspect, Tamerlan Tsarnaev, is killed in police confrontation. His brother, suspect Dzhokhar Tsarnaev, is arrested and charged with one count of using and attempting to use a mass destruction weapon resulting in death and one count of malicious destruction of property by an explosive device resulting in death. He gets death sentence on June 25, 2015.

16 July 2015 – Mohammad Abdulazeez is setting fire to a military recruitment center and naval reserve base in Chattanooga, Tennessee, killing four U.S. Marines and a naval sailor. Abdulazeez dies in compliance gunfight. FBI Director James Comey later said Abdulazeez 'acts were "motivated by propaganda from international terrorist groups," adding that it's difficult to decide which terrorist group may have influenced him.

2 December 2015 – Married couple Syed Rizwan Farook and Tashfeen Malik open fire at an Inland Regional Center holiday party in San Bernardino, California, killing 14 people. A police shootout kills Farook and Malik. Investigators assume the couple's self-radicalized.

12 June 2016 – Omar Mateen, an American-born man who had vowed loyalty to ISIS, is killing 49 people and injuring others in a shooting spree at a gay nightclub in Orlando, the second-deadliest mass shooting in modern U.S. history, and the nation's worst terror attack since 9/11. Fire and kill Mateen inside the bar.

12 August 2017 — One person is killed and 19 injured when a speeding car crashes into a throng of demonstrators in Charlottesville, Virginia, where a "Unite the Right" rally of white nationalists and other far-right groups was organized to protest the city's decision to remove a Confederate Gen. Robert E. Lee statue. James Alex Fields Jr., is convicted in December 2018 by a first-degree murder jury in Virginia and nine other charges, pleading guilty to 29 federal hate crimes in March 2019. Fields are later convicted by both a Virginia state judge and a federal judge to life imprisonment, with two terms

running consecutively. President Donald Trump signs a bipartisan "joint resolution condemning abuse and domestic terrorist attack" in Charlottesville on September 14, 2017.

October 31, 2017 – Eight people are killed and nearly a dozen wounded when a 29-year-old man drives down a crowded bicycle path near New York's World Trade Centre. The defendant is Sayfullo Habibullaevic Saipov. Saipov is later charged with 28 counts, including eight murder charges, 18 attempted murder charges, and other terrorism allegations.

August 3, 2019 — Twenty-two people are killed in El Paso, Texas following a mass shooting in a Walmart store classified as domestic terrorism. Police claim they discovered an anti-immigrant document promoting white nationalist and racist beliefs written by the suspect, 21-year-old Patrick Crusius. Crusius is later charged with death and federal hate crime as well as weapons offences.

December 6, 2019 — A gunman killed three U.S. sailors at a Naval Air Station in Pensacola, Florida. The gunman, identified as Mohammed Alshamrani, a 21-year-old

Royal Saudi Air Force second lieutenant and student naval flight officer, is killed in a gunfire exchange with two deputies. At a news conference on January 13, 2020, Attorney General William Barr said the shooting was a terrorist act inspired by "jihadist ideology." The FBI revealed on May 18, 2020, evidence from the killer's phone suggested that he was a long-time al-Qaeda member who had connected with group operatives as recently as the night before the shooting.

Two shooters attack a Kosher grocery store in Jersey City, New Jersey, killing three people inside the shop. New Jersey Attorney General Gurbir S. Grewal later said the killings are being investigated as domestic terrorism, "fuelled by anti-Semitism and anti-law enforcement views." Before committing the killings at the shop, the gunmen killed a police officer near a cemetery in Jersey City. The gunmen David N. Anderson, 47, and Francine Graham, 50, die in a police standoff.

Despite the increased focus on international terrorism, it's important to remain aware of the full spectrum of threats facing the U.S. These threats include domestic and foreign terrorists. While the majority of domestic terrorist attacks have yielded low casualty estimates, the 169 lives reported in the Oklahoma City bombing and the possible very heavy loss of life that could have resulted from numerous thwarted plots indicate the interest of certain domestic extremists in causing mass casualties.

On September 11, 2001, the complexity and magnitude of the international radical jihad movement was seen with horrific clarity when 19 hijackers controlled four commercial airliners, crashing two of them into the World Trade Center, one into the Pentagon, and the other into a remote Pennsylvania area. This attack resulted in more deaths than any terrorist act ever reported.

While the Al-Qaeda command structure in Afghanistan is being dismantled, Al-Qaeda cells in countries around the world will continue to target U.S. The plotters who carried out the September 11, 2001 attack kept a low profile and seemed to deliberately avoid the attention of law enforcement officials. Such organizational discipline underlines the challenge for U.S. law enforcement officials to expose and disrupt U.S. Al-Qaeda cells. While the public mind frequently group foreign terrorists into a common stereotype, this view fails to accept subtle yet significant variations in aims and strategies between different radical groups. For example, 17 November's low-level operational reach (assassinations, small-scale bombings focused primarily in Athens) reflects the organization's narrow, ethnocentric strategic aim (a nationalist Greek state). By comparison, Al-Qaeda 's high-impact, transnational tactical orientation and other organizations affiliated with the international radical jihad movement clearly underlines a strategic aim to target the U.S. and other Western interests with high-casualty terrorist attacks. Despite Al-Qaeda 's military defeats, extremists adhering to the international jihad movement will continue to concentrate on attacks that produce major damage and high casualties, increasing worldwide media coverage and public fear. It also seems likely that as governments "harden" (or make more secure) official targets, such as embassies and international schools, these terrorists will gradually pursue more vulnerable "softer" targets, such as high-profile multinational corporate offices and Americans traveling and working abroad.

Chapter 6: HISTORY OF THE DEEP STATE SINCE THE FIRST US PRESIDENT

Nearly two years after the "deep state" became part of the American lexicon. In early February 2017, just weeks after President Donald Trump's inauguration, news outlets first reported the word's growing use in the president's inner circle. Over the following months, his administration's president and backers openly embellished the deep state's meaning and importance, rendering it a catchphrase for alleged internal enemies in Washington. News analysis of the phenomenon has done a lot to shed light on how the perspective of right-wing activists like Steve Bannon and Alex Jones has helped to bring administration supporters to the idea of "deep state." Although the phrase has caused a lot of circumspection in political media, it is now clear that the notion of a deep state has gained some relevance to the American public. According to a spring 2018 Monmouth poll, 37% of respondents knew about something called the deep state. When asked whether they

69

believed that "a network of unelected government and military officials secretly controlling or guiding national policy" existed, nearly three-quarters of respondents agreed to such a "deep state."

I have been interested in the idea of a deep state for some time now. As a Turkish Republic historian, I have first introduced the word almost 20 years ago as a graduate student. When I first visited Turkey in the early 2000s, someone who talked about the deep state did not do so facially or objectively. Serious people not only acknowledged the presence of a deep Turkish state, but they also seemed to believe it was an essential factor that characterized Turkey's history. Most of my research has been devoted to understanding many people, organizations, and events affiliated with the deep Turkish state for over a decade. Among the works that motivated me to look deeper at Turkey's deep state phenomenon were books and articles written by Peter Dale Scott, a Canadian diplomat-turned professor. His 1993 novel, published by JFK's University of California Press, Deep Politics and Death, caught my attention as a few scholarly studies to frame American history in a light close to deep-state Turkish discussions. In 2007, I had the opportunity to interview Scott on a (thankfully) short-lived podcast I released as a professor at Long Island University. Our discussion took place within weeks of his latest thesis, The Road to 9/11, in which he first used the word "deep state." As a result of this book, and the attention he later got from Alex Jones and others, many Americans first entertained the idea that a deep state lorded over the U.S.

What follows is not an attempt to discuss or describe the nature of the deep state, but to trace the history of how and why the term entered American speech. It's a tale that starts first in Turkey, where the word was first coined and built on how scholars and commentators applied it elsewhere. How Peter Dale Scott learned of the concept and applying it to the United States is instructive about ideas and drawbacks that have long characterized the concept's development. Conspiracies within government or the possibility of collaboration can be found in most countries' annals, including the United States. Revelations of these schemes have also led observers to believe that hidden cabals are central to a nation's affairs, creating structures for themselves. Aspects of Turkish culture and cases elsewhere, suggest such a phenomenon is not the product of imagination. Yet identifying what is a deep state, let alone recording its nature, is another matter. The tale of how the deep state penetrated American consciousness highlights the flawed science and fiction that hinders any discussion of hidden societies and shadow regimes.

Turkey: The Ur Deep State?

Modern Turkey's creation can not be addressed without remembering its history of governmental conspiracies. Conspiratorial parties and activities are at the center of many significant events that shaped the world's modern history. For example, it is abundantly clear that the Republic of Turkey was founded by individuals who helped form a true "state within a state" during the Ottoman Empire's later years. Mustafa Kemal Atatürk, the country's founder, was among the Union and Development Committee (CUP) founding members, the political party that governed the empire in its final decade. While the CUP upheld the façade of being an open party committed to parliamentary government and the rule of law, its members maintained a secret parallel country control system.

As the empire entered its final throes of collapse, the CUP relied on its clandestine arms to maintain power and eliminate perceived state threats. Among the chief actions connected with this secret power system was the Armenian genocide, partially conducted with the assistance of paramilitaries and related civilian loyalists. While Atatürk may have remained aloof from the government's anti-Armenian policies, covert CUP operatives proved instrumental in promoting his rise to the Republic's establishment in 1923.

For some historians, the CUP period contributed to the creation of the Turkish state's culture of intrigue and subversion. Repeated military coups that wrecked Turkey in the 20th century are often depicted as a legacy of the CUP's reliance on cabals within the Ottoman army to maintain its grip on the empire. Of all the events that have epitomized the position of hidden factions in Turkish history, the so-called 1996 Susurluk Incident is the clearest and most vivid case of clandestine actors' enduring strength. The case, which revealed the government's recruitment of gangsters as hitmen to pursue its dirty war against the Kurdish Workers Party (PKK), seemed to point to a wider mistreatment and abuse trend within Turkey's political establishment. Susurluk seemed to indicate that the elected government was merely a shell that concealed the country's true rulers' identity, a collection of military, intelligence, mafia, and business elite members. This alliance's goal, it was generally assumed, was simple: kill or discredit anyone they believed threatened the Turkish state and nation's integrity. The covert, extralegal existence of this supposed system was central to what most people believed was Turkey's deep state.

The Susurluk incident helped popularize the "deep state" theory, but did not actually spawn its definition. It's not entirely clear today who invented the term or when it was first used. While some argued that it was first used by leftist commentators before 1996, one journalist claimed that the first phrase originated from the government minister's mouth, who helped recruit the Susurluk assassins. Regardless of its precise origin, by the beginning of the new century, the term became an integral part of Turkish vocabulary. However, there was little consensus as to exactly who or what constituted the deep Turkish state, widespread fear over the presence of a parallel structure of governmental authority was one of the most important factors leading to Recep Tayyip Erdoğan's 2002 Justice and Development Party (AKP) victory. As prime minister, Erdogan promised a "clean hands" approach to government and vowed to eliminate the deep state that had existed since the Ottomans' last days. In 2008, it seemed he had begun keeping this vow. Over the next few years, prosecutors charged a single underground group called Ergenekon, which was behind a series of conspiracies to overthrow and influence the Turkish state. The origins of this cartel, allegedly comprising senior military officers, officials, politicians, gangsters, and journalists, were described as decades-old, dating back to events even before the Susurluk scandal.

Convictions in the Ergenekon trial were widely heralded to signify that the deep state finally met its match (promoted by Erdogan himself). Even then, critics raised questions about the legitimacy of the government argument, casting it as an attempt to undermine the AKP administration opponents. Ahmet Šık, a prominent investigative journalist, was among the first to say that the Ergenekon investigation was an undertaking orchestrated by police and state attorneys loyal to a religious movement orchestrated by Fethullah Gülen, a U.S.-based cleric then allying Erdogan's government. The eventual split between Erdogan and Gülen, which may have sparked the attempted July 2016 coup, did much to confuse what the Turkish deep state meant. According to state prosecutors and many pro-Erdogan commentators today, Gülen and his adherents allegedly dominated Turkey's deep state for a long time (a partisans claim, substantiated by the 2016 coup as well as Gülenists' positions in prosecuting the Ergenekon trials). Ahmet Sik, now a member of parliament, responded that the AKP had eventually bested Gülen in a fight for deep state power, leading to "a mafia sultanate" run by Erdogan himself.

Today 's discussion on Turkey's deep state represents long-simmering disputes over how the term is understood. Scholars or commentators have been grappling with the true meaning of the deep state since 1996 and the specifics that characterized its creation during republic history. For example, there is broad consensus that a covert NATO-led unit called Operation Gladio had heavily influenced the Turkish deep state. As a covert group in the Turkish state ranks, Gladio was suspected of being an independently run "stay-behind army" to fight alleged communists and other presumed subversives in a war with the Soviet Union. For scholars, how influential this unit was in shaping Turkey's deep state, let alone how it developed over time, has long remained somewhat elusive. Worsening the discussion about its importance is the virtual lack of verifiable government reports referring to the group's presence or activities.

Press interviews with supposed witnesses and members of this "counter-guerrilla" program, instead of hard facts, provided the bulk of information. Testimony from hearsay and unreliable sources also covered up state-run inquiries into Susurluk and Ergenekon events. It is now painfully clear that investigators in the Ergenekon investigation produced testimony and relied heavily on confidential or dubious witness accounts. Official government departments in Turkey have not helped answer concerns about the country's deep state history. There is no formal state record declassification scheme in Turkey. Except for archives operated by prime minister's office, none of the country's key ministries provide easy public access to their records.

Turkey's internal debates on its supposed deep state initially prompted only a few scholars to look for deep states in other countries. Scholars used the term as a jump-off point to examine a select number of events, such as the implementation of military rule in Cold War Greece and the army's continuing power and bureaucracy over the Thai government. The protests that erupted in Cairo's Tahrir Square in 2011, following the overthrow of Mohammed Morsi's Muslim Brotherhood regime, prompted many similarities between Egypt's deep state and Turkey's. Osama bin Laden's discovery in May 2011 prompted others to apply the deep state nickname to Pakistan's intelligence agency, the ISI, due to its Karachi impact. The first academic attempt to internationalize the deep-state idea came in a 2009 essay by Norwegian scholar Ola Tunander. In reading a series of terrorist attacks committed by members of the Italian clandestine service during the height of the Cold War, Tunander argued that the deep state (regardless of where one may find it) is simply a feature of what Hans Morgenthau had previously called the current "dual state." As an institution independent from the open, officially recognized "democratic" state, the deep stable. As elected governments challenge the domestic or foreign interests of the deep state, actors associated with this alliance (which Tunander associates with the military, intelligence service, mafia, and far-right political activists) use every means to change the state's political path.

Tunander articulated this deep-state view before a 2006 Melbourne conference. The case, dedicated to studying "parapolitics and shadow governance," featured many well-respected organized crime scholars and numerous regional fields. Except for Tunander, none of the participants used the word "deep state" in their presentations. Some scholars preferred similar conceptual concepts, such as "parapolitics," a more general phrase used to characterize the relationships between state actors and nefarious groups in institution. The writer, perhaps best known for popularizing "parapolitics," Peter Dale Scott, was attending the meeting. Hitherto, Scott later explained, he had never heard of the deep state, but was taken elsewhere by Tunander 's study of Italy and its applicability. "I was really happy," he told me in 2007 to know "how closely, how closely, my study of America matched Ola Tunander's [thinking] of America and other states."

Chapter 7: THROUGH THE LOOKING GLASS: THE DEEP STATE COMES TO AMERICA

As a literature professor at Berkeley's University of California, Peter Dale Scott's participation in anti-war politics produced his scholarship's first light. His advocacy culminated in 1972 when his first book, The War Plan, was published, alleging that the U.S. intelligence community had helped push Washington into Vietnam 's invasion. His continued interest in the war's history soon sparked greater interest in the Kennedy assassination, as many activists pointed out as a turning point in America's participation in Southeast Asia. Scott kept publishing his research on Kennedy, releasing an edited volume on Iran-Contra and the role cocaine smugglers played in the scandal. When Deep Politics and JFK's Death was published by University of California Press, Oliver Stone's cinematic treatment of the assassination had come and gone to theaters, sparking a groundswell of concern. But, unlike most of the contentious films, Deep Politics invests no energy contesting what is exposed in the

Zapruder film or discussing the merits of the "magic bullet theory." The assassination, as Scott would have it, opened windows to a range of topics otherwise concealed from public view. The Warren Commission, as well as Congress' re-examination of the 1976 inquiry, provided a treasure trove of insights into the CIA's relationship with organized crime and its monitoring efforts within the United States. In analyzing the biographies and incidents associated with the shooting, Scott points to a multitude of movements trying to undo Kennedy's policies, intensify the Cold War, and other causes of right-wing. Although highlighting the value of the hidden forces that theoretically benefited from the assassination, Deep Politics provides no clear alternative to what happened in Dealey Plaza. "You can't solve the case," Scott said in 2007, "but by researching the case, we can learn more about America."

Instead of discarding Oswald and unmasking JFK's real killers, Deep Politics draws from the assassination a much wider historical lesson. Kennedy's death, in Scott's opinion, wasn't a random, external plot that hit America. It was more likely to be a "systemic change" intended to circumvent

Kennedy's tendencies toward political reform at home and military de-escalation abroad. While not naming the plot, Scott hypothesizes that a great alliance of powers contained inside "public government, organized crime, and private money" orchestrated and gained from the president's death. Deep Politics muses that JFK's killing was only one episode in a series of cases that contributed to the continuation of the Cold War and the protection of unliberal policies at home (cases that may have included Watergate and Iran-Contra). Yet for whatever "parapolitics" or "deep politics" residing behind the Kennedy assassination and other contentious incidents, Scott provides no definite ruling on what to term this parallel authority source.

Ultimately, his participation in the 2006 Melbourne conference gave him a more suitable diction for what he sought to explain in Deep Politics. While attending the event to discuss his work on drug trafficking and politics in Mexico, he noticed a novel concept in Ola Tunander 's paper that could be applied to a new research project he had started. In The Path to 9/11: Riches, Power, and America's Future, Scott identifies

America's deep state as the possibly complicit author and primary beneficiary of the 2001 assault. As in Deep Politics, he provides no alternate explanation for what occurred on 9/11 (although he supports the work of David Ray Griffin and others who argue that the attacks were the result of a plot beyond al-Qaeda). Instead, he spends much of the book charting the history of covert U.S. interference abroad and how these policies helped establish Osama bin Laden. For Scott, the undercover players who helped lay al-Qaeda's foundations were the same as those who helped push and manipulate U.S. foreign policy after the Cold War (specifically, U.S. intelligence, oil industry, and organized crime).

Similarly, Washington's response to 9/11 was the result of the historical growth of the deep state. In discussing the Patriot Act and Guantanamo's roots, Scott claims that the Bush administration (mainly Dick Cheney and Donald Rumsfeld) supported similar policies from the 1970s. Among the more jolting arguments of The Path to 9/11 is the belief that Cheney and Rumsfeld had helped form Reagan's "government stability" strategy, pushing for the Constitution's suspension and the establishment of FEMA-run internment camps in the event of a national crisis. Elements of this initiative were enacted on or after 9/11.

The path to 9/11 was published as a peer-reviewed monograph by University of California Press. Both works are highly noted. While some government documents provide the basis for his facts, Scott primarily relies on the reporting of investigative journalists and other media outlets as the base of his research. To date, very few academic journals have published book reviews (of the few that exist, Ola Tunander offered the work's brightest evaluation). Academia's ambivalent book reception did nothing to weaken the book's visibility elsewhere. Scott first appeared on Alex Jones' radio show, Infowars, in February 2008. By then, Alex Jones had just become a global phenomenon. Jones' argument that the 9/11 attacks were an "inside job" had already created a "truther" movement aimed at revealing the involvement of the CIA, the Mossad, and foreign industrialists (mainly those affiliated with the Bilderberg Group) in the attack. Scott's findings immediately linked this line of thinking. He then appeared to live on Infowars and published articles on the show's website. Other contributors to Alex Jones' brand quickly started incorporating the deep state into their study of the Obama administration and the overall U.S. government. By 2016, Infowars prophesied that Donald Trump was the man most likely to destroy the deep state that one analyst likened to a "satanic coalition" of capitalists, "corporatists," and representatives of the military-industrial complex of America. The deep state only became a staple of Steve Bannon's news site, Breitbart, a month after election day. In a long survey detailing what the author suggested will be a forthcoming battle between "The Deep State vs. Donald Trump," an anonymous reader, Virgil (who some commentators believe to be Bannon), portrayed the deep American state as a vast informal government containing untold thousands of "bureaucrats, technocrats and plutocrats" dedicated to keeping President-elect Trump out of the power "It stretches across the federal government, indeed the whole country," Virgil warned. "And it involves not only politicians, but also a galaxy of private-sector vendors, profiteers, and others."

It can be noted that in the American context, scholars other than Peter Dale

Scott had similar theories to the deep state. As early as 2014, Tufts University Professor Michael Glennon gave the phrase "double government" in evaluating the remaining national security agencies spanning the Bush and Obama administration. Continuities between Bush and Obama, he claimed, showed that the country had "moved beyond a mere imperial presidency to a bifurcated regime – a double-government framework – in which even the president now retains no substantive influence over the overall course of U.S. national security policy." And he never paints America's double government as wedded to cartels or multinational corporations. Nor does he take incidents like the JFK assassination as evidence of the double government's life.

At this point, "double government" is unlikely to invoke the same power and sense as a deep state. Since Spring 2017, the deep state has been deeply embedded in America's political language as the main term synonymous with alternative power structures or covert politics. Attempts to describe the content have since ranged from genuinely serious efforts to sheer mockery. Last year, the word acquired a highly political connotation within the United States. At least four of President Trump's most prominent backers have written deep-state book-length accounts to discredit his administration. Scott, meanwhile, has continued to write and give interviews on the subject, saying recently that he hopes "Trump and the deep state can make the other more moderate."

Looking Back to Look Forward

If the debates since February 2017 have done something, it is to underline contradictions that have long beset the ideological tradition of the deep state. Although it was coined over 20 years ago, no clear description of what it means has taken place. Using the term commonly denotes belief in an informal or parallel government to circumvent legal, normally more representative, institutions. Who forms this shadow government mainly depends on who you ask, and when or when the debate takes place. While the word originated in reference to the control security institutions has over state and society (such as in Turkey), the list of deep state actors may include social groups suspected of manipulating everyday citizens, such as mafia, "big business," or ideological extremists.

Extreme political incidents were typically catalysts for those who thought the word appropriate or beneficial until February 2017. In other words, "it's the deep state" acted as a brief response to those who doubt the true roots of any number of unusual, typically violent episodes: Susurluk, the JFK assassination, 9/11, etc. Interestingly, the coming of the deep state to America is that it was used so pre-emptively. For analysts who now use the word literally, the deep American state cares because it is capable of unseating President Donald Trump and not simply because of what it did before. Whether academics will continue to debate, the deep state remains to be seen. Given the partisan political radioactivity that enveloped the term, most reputable scholars would probably think twice before distilling or confirming a deep state.

What also seems to suggest is the degree to which the hunt for shadow governments has always been elusive. There are several historical cases pointing to covert agendas and hidden cabals within governments. Documenting and contextualizing such conspiracies is not necessarily motivated by wild-eyed hysteria or political agendas. In the U.S. case, government corruption allegations have caused significant public disclosures. For example, widespread skepticism about the JFK assassination prompted Congress to launch a new investigation, leading to startling official revelations of the CIA's domestic surveillance activities and recruiting American mafia elements. Whether such leaks are indicative of systematic political cabals or shadow regimes is frequently questioned by deep-state discussions. Proposing that a deep systemic state exists means that several individuals and organizations coordinate with each other (harmoniously or otherwise) through years and shifts in staff and regimes. Making such an argument becomes much more fraught when one extends the scope of deep state players to include broad categories such as media, organized crime, or "big oil." One point is that bureaucracies may resist reform or assume that private people or organizations may secretly manipulate legislators. Such interests form distinct collectives that can span decades or centuries without changing or breaking down. Assuming a deep state is a permanent fixture within states may lead one to construe it as an actual entity with a constant cast of individuals meeting and planning over long periods. At best, the prospects for demonstrating such a parallel state in the form of government or objective testimony are questionable. More often than not, the quest for a deep state helps those trying to conflate and marginalize political critics and opponents.

One lesson to be gleaned from deep state conceptual growth concerns transparency. At the heart of the deep state's rhetorical appeal is a mistrust of government, particularly governments (or parts thereof), which are assumed to be less than forthcoming. The clandestine or closed existence of many organizations commonly associated with the term, such as military and intelligence services, increases concerns of deeper conspiracies. One way to address the cause of such suspicions is to ensure that state records are publicly accessible and managed inconsistent and straightforward ways. For the United States, mandating the publication of all state records after normal periods is one potential remedy (as seen in Britain's "twenty-year rule"). Such a system will remove much of the paperwork, cost, and uncertainty that plagues researchers and archivists using College Park, Maryland's National Archive. However, the possibility of Washington's politicians being comfortable authorizing greater public access to state documents is certainly slim. While changes under Obama, the declassification of current and historical records remain incomplete. In addition to official apprehensions regarding revealing previously kept information, Congress has repeatedly cut the National Archive's budget (archive operating expenditure fell 8 percent between 2008 and 2018). Any increase in the archive's budget, not to mention enhancing public access, will be a subtle but important step to restore public faith in state institutions and help battle the mistrust that undergirds believe in the deep state.

Chapter 8: THE ILLUMINATI

Who's Illuminati?

Adam Weishaupt, an anti-clerical professor who wanted to restrict the Church's involvement in public life, created the original Illuminati party in 18th century Bavaria.

Convinced that religious beliefs were no longer an appropriate belief structure for ruling modern societies, "he wanted to find another type of 'illumination;' a collection of beliefs and practices that could be implemented to fundamentally change how European states were operated," National Geographic reports. He based his secret society on the Freemasons, with a hierarchy and enigmatic rituals, and called it the Illuminati Order to represent its educated members' enlightened ideals.

Chris Hodapp, co-author of Conspiracy Theories and Secret Societies for Dummies, says a distinguishing characteristic of early Illuminati members is that they didn't trust anyone over 30 because they were so set in their ways.

Historians prefer to think that the original Illuminati was just "mildly successful — at best — in being powerful," says Vox. The order boasted several prominent members, the most famous being the German theorist Johann Goethe.

A government crackdown on secret societies in the late 1780s stamped the Illuminati out, but reports that it continued to exist as an underground group persisted into the modern era.

Among the supposed secret society members are not only politicians, religious figures, but also celebrities and pop stars.

The Illuminati theory has no small number of dedicated adherents, particularly in the US-according to Insider 's survey, about 15 percent of the American electorate believe the Illuminati exist.

The news site reports the most likely age groups were Gen X-ers and older millennials, and "Republicans were more likely to believe in secret society than Democrats."

"In 2016, an estimated 200 million Americans were registered to vote," the site states. "If Insider 's survey were an accurate image of the entire U.S. population, 30 million of those voters will be Illuminati believers."

How did the modern-day myth develop?

The book celebrated an alternative belief system — Discordianism — that advocated a type of anarchism and gave rise to the Discordian movement that eventually sought to trigger civil disobedience through practical jokes and hoaxes.

One of the key advocates of this new philosophy was a writer named Robert Anton Wilson who tried to return anarchy to society through "disseminating disinformation through all channels – through counter-culture, through mass media," Bramwell says.

He did this by sending fake letters to the men's Playboy magazine where he worked, attributing cover-ups and conspiracy theories like the JFK assassination to a secret elite group called the Illuminati.

Wilson turned these theories into a book, The Illuminatus Trilogy, which became a surprise cult success and became a stage play in Liverpool, launching British actors Bill Nighy and Jim Broadbent's careers.

What is the New World Order?

The notion of a strong modern Illuminati plotting to conquer the planet remained a fringe concept maintained until the 1990s by a few enthusiasts.

The internet changed all that, offering conspiracy theorists a worldwide forum to express their theories to a large audience.

Theories on how the Modern World Order works range from reasonably simple theories to the surreal.

Conspiracy theorists obsessively examine public events for Illuminati-influence "proof." The symbols most associated with the Illuminati include circles, pentagrams, pigs, the all-seeing eye — like the one on US banknotes — and number 666.

This led to suggestions that some of the American Founding Fathers were members, accusing Thomas Jefferson during the War of Independence.

Another widely cited Illuminati emblem found on US currency is the so-called Eye of Providence, which is claimed to represent God's omniscience watching over humanity.

According to a 2013 Public Policy Polling survey, 28 percent of U.S. voters believe a hidden power elite with a globalist agenda is plotting to ultimately dominate the planet through an oppressive global government. It found that 34 percent of Republicans and 35 percent of independents believe in the New World Order threat, compared to just 15% of Democrats.

Who's a suspected member?

Besides becoming king and queen of posters, Beyonce and Jay-Z are also represented as New World Order rulers. Beyonce's enormous wealth and popularity made her a favorite target for conspiracy theorists.

Illuminati's "experts" took her half-time appearance at the 2013 Super Bowl as an example of her "devil-worshipping" choreography, even accusing Sasha Fierce of being a "demonic being" on stage.

Some musicians, however, seem to enjoy playing with symbols related to secret societies.

For example, Rihanna often integrates Illuminati imagery into her music videos and even jokes about the theories in S&M 's video, featuring a fake newspaper with a headline calling her "Princess of the Illuminati."

Often accused of hiding hidden symbols like devil horns and goat imagery in his music videos. The logo for his own music label, Roc-A-Fella Records, is a pyramid, one of Illuminati's most famous logos.

Rob Brotherton, author of Suspicious Minds and a professor at Barnard College: Why We Believe in Conspiracy Theories, explains that real-life government conspiracies targeting black people in America, such as FBI infiltration of the Civil Rights movement in the 1950s and 60s, planted seeds for the popularity of Illuminati theory among artists and fans.

Speaking to Complex, he said: "Hip-hop acted as this [soapbox] for people to speak about problems important to them, such as segregation, racism, the criminal justice system, mostly seemingly aimed at African-Americans."

"It's a fast hop from witnessing any injustice to worrying about whether there's something behind it. Hip-hop was just a strong candidate to revive this theory.

What do celebrities think about theories?

Katy Perry told Rolling Stone in 2014 that the idea was the creation of "weird people on the internet," but acknowledged that she was flattered to be listed among the purported members: "I guess you've made it when they think you 're in the Illuminati!" She added that she was respectful of those who wanted to believe the idea because: "I believe in aliens."

On the other hand, Madonna may just be a believer – all the more fascinating because she was always accused of being a fake. Speaking to Rolling Stone, she indicated the group's hidden intelligence. The assertion is not so surprising as she released a single, 'Illuminati.' She said: "People always accuse me of being an Illuminati member, but I know who the Illuminati are."

In February 2016, Beyonce shocked her fans by releasing a new song, Formation — but conspiracy theorists were excited for another reason. The track's very first line admitted rumors: "You haters corny with that Illuminati mess."

When Prince died unexpectedly of an accidental overdose in April of the same year, a small but vocal corner of the internet accused the Illuminati of killing the singer-songwriter, who was known for fiercely defending his copyright and creative freedom from interference with industry.

"The Illuminati talk will not stop coming, and what does not help is that Prince himself seems to be fully persuaded that the group existed," one gossip website notes.

The singer appeared on TV in 2009 warning of powerful mystery figures controlling the world via "chemtrails"—chemicals injected into the air through jet planes to influence human behavior.

Chapter 9: TERRORISTIC ATTACKS

The 9/11 terrorist attack marked a drastic acceleration in a trend towards more devastating terrorist attacks that started in the 1980s. Before the attack on September 11, the truck bombings of U.S. and French military barracks in Beirut, Lebanon, which took 295 lives, were the most deadly terrorist act. The September 11 attacks created casualty estimates more than ten times higher than the 1983 barrack attacks.

The 9/11 attack also represented a move towards more indiscriminate targeting by foreign terrorists. The overwhelming majority of the attack's casualties were civilians. Moreover, the attack was the first known case of suicide bombings by foreign terrorists in the U.S. The September 11 attack also marked the first successful U.S. act of international terrorism since the World Trade Center vehicle bombing in February 1993.

In its unparalleled reach and devastation, the 9/11 attack exposed many of the international terrorism patterns reported in recent years by the U.S. intelligence community (Central Intelligence Agency, National Security Agency, Defense Intelligence Agency, State Department Bureau of Intelligence and Research, Defense Department intelligence elements, Treaties). Among these were an obvious change in tactical strength from conventional terrorist sources — state sponsors and formalized terrorist organizations — to loosely linked extremists. This pattern paralleled a general change in strategies and methodologies among foreign terrorists focused on mass casualties. These patterns underline the serious threat posed by foreign terrorists to nations worldwide, particularly the United States.

Simultaneously, the U.S. also faces major threats from domestic terrorists. The FBI reported 335 attacks or alleged terror attacks in this country between 1980 and 2000. Of these, 247 were linked to domestic terrorists, while 88 were foreign.

Threats from domestic and foreign terrorists will continue to pose a major threat for the near future. Furthermore, as terrorists continue to refine and extend their methodologies, the threats they pose will increase.

Background

The FBI divides America's terrorist threat into two broad categories — domestic and international.

Domestic terrorism is the threatened or unlawful use of violence by a group or entity based and operating entirely within the United States (or its territories) without any international direction perpetrated against persons or property to intimidate or coerce a government, a civilian population, or any section thereof in the pursuit of political goals.

International terrorism includes violent actions or activities dangerous to human life that violate the U.S. or any state's criminal laws, or that may be a criminal violation if committed within the U.S. or any state's jurisdiction. Acts aim to threaten or coerce a civilian population, influence a government's policy, or affect a government's conduct. These actions cross national borders as to how they are done, the individuals they are intended to threaten, or the place where the perpetrators work.

As events over the past few years indicate, domestic and foreign terrorist groups pose threats to Americans inside U.S. borders.

The nature of the terrorist threat has changed significantly over the past decade. In the 1990s, the most serious domestic extremist threat to the nation was left-wing extremism. As characterized by the Animal Liberation Front (ALF) and the Earth Liberation Front (ELF), significant interest in extremism has emerged in recent years as a serious terrorist danger. The FBI reports that since 1996, ALF / ELF has committed about 600 illegal acts in the United States, resulting in damages of $42 million.

However, as the events of September 11 revealed with awful clarity, the U.S. still faces severe threats from foreign terrorists. Usama Bin Laden's transnational Al-Qaeda terrorist network has emerged as the most immediate threat to U.S. interests. The evidence linking Bin Laden and Al-Qaeda to the 9/11 attacks are strong and irrefutable. U.S. law enforcement and military intervention have done much to disrupt Al-Qaeda's organizational structure and capabilities. Despite Al-Qaeda 's military setbacks, however, it must continue to be seen as a strong, highly capable terrorist network with cells worldwide. Al-Qaeda is wounded at this trial, but not dead; down but not out.

Over the past decade, the FBI has worked actively to improve its capacity to deter and prosecute terrorist attacks against U.S. interests wherever planned. The FBI operates 44 Legal Attache (Legats) offices worldwide to help ensure that investigative tools are in place to support the FBI's growing focus on counter-terrorism and international organized crime. In the 20 years since President Reagan named the FBI as the lead counter-terrorism agency in the U.S., Congress and the Executive Branch have taken crucial measures to strengthen the federal government's counter-terrorism capabilities. The FBI's anti-terrorism duties were extended in 1984 and 1986 when Congress passed legislation allowing the Bureau to exercise federal authority overseas when terrorists kidnap, threaten, or ransom a U.S. citizen, or when certain U.S. interests are threatened. The FBI investigated over 500 extraterritorial cases since the mid-1980s. In addition to investigating the September 11 attack, several other active extraterritorial investigations rank among the FBI's highest-profile cases, including our 1996 bombing of Khobar Towers in Saudi Arabia, which killed 19 U.S. servicemen; U.S. bombings. Embassies in Kenya and Tanzania killed 12 Americans; and the USS Cole bombing, which killed 17 U.S. sailors.

As demonstrated by our improved capacity to conduct counter-terrorism investigations abroad, the FBI's approach to terrorism matured over the past decade reflects the growing nature of terrorism. Following the 1993 World Trade Center bombing, the FBI began focusing investigative attention on Sunni extremism's then-emerging phenomenon and its organizational expression in the radical international jihad movement. In the summer of 1993, investigators discovered and disrupted an attempt by a loosely linked group of foreign terrorists headed by Shaykh Omar Abdel Rahman to bomb landmarks across New York City.

This morning, I would like to briefly discuss the current U.S. terrorist threat and the FBI's attempts to counter the danger posed by domestic and foreign terrorists.

Terrorist Threat in the United States

Despite robust law enforcement measures and major legislative counter-terrorism legislation, the U.S. terrorist threat persists. The total incidence of terrorist-related incidents in the U.S. decreased in the early 1990s relative to estimates in the 1970s and 1980s but has gradually risen over the past five years. The United States reported two terrorist attacks in 1995, three in 1996, four in 1997, five in 1995, 12 in 1999, and 8 in 2000 (FIGURES COMBINE TERRORIST INCIDENTS AND Alleged TERRORIST INCIDENTS). Although terrorist designations for 2001 are currently being finalized, one incident, September 11's attack, created higher casualty figures than all previous terrorist incidents combined in the United States. In recent years, relatively large numbers of terrorist attacks thwarted by law enforcement further underline the current terrorist threat.

Domestic Terrorism

Domestic right-wing extremist organizations also adopt white discrimination ideals and promote anti-government, anti-regulatory views. Extremist right-wing groups typically participate in conduct secured by constitutional guarantees of free expression and assembly. Law enforcement becomes involved when these groups' unpredictable talk transgresses into illegal action.

At national level, organized right-wing hate organizations such as the National Alliance, the World Creator Church (WCOTC) and the Aryan Nations pose an active terrorist threat. While some radical groups have made attempts to minimize overtly racist language to appeal to a wider segment of the population and concentrate on anti-government sentiment, racism-based hate remains an integral component of these organizations' core orientations.

Right-wing extremists pose a significant terrorist threat. Two of the seven attempted terrorist acts thwarted in 1999 were potentially large-scale, high-casualty attacks plotted by right-wing militant groups.

The second category of domestic terrorists, left-wing organizations, typically adopt a revolutionary socialist ideology and see themselves as protectors of the people against capitalism and imperialism's "dehumanizing impact." They strive to bring about change in the U.S. and believe this change can be achieved by revolution rather than the existing democratic process. From the 1960s to the 1980s, leftist-oriented militant groups faced America's most significant domestic terrorist threat. But the socialist movement's fortunes shifted drastically in the 1980s when law enforcement destroyed many of these groups' structures. The collapse of communism in Eastern Europe stripped the movement of its intellectual base and patronage.

Terrorist groups demanding complete Puerto Rican independence from the U.S. by violent means are among the few active vestiges of left-wing extremism. Although these groups believe bombings alone will not change, they see these acts of terrorism as a way of bringing attention to their desire for freedom. Numerous radical organizations, including militant Puerto Rican nationalist groups such as the Puerto Rican National Liberation Army (FALN — Fuerzas Armadas de Liberacion Nacional Puertorriquena), carried out bombings on the U.S. mainland, mostly in and around New York City. However, just as the leftist threat typically decreased significantly in the 1990s, Puerto Rican terrorist groups' danger to mainland U.S. communities has diminished throughout the past decade.

However, terrorist attacks remain committed by militant separatists in Puerto Rico. As reported, over the past four years, three terrorist acts and one alleged terrorist attack have occurred in different Puerto Rican locations. These actions (including the March 31 1998 bombing of a superaquaduct project in Arecibo, the June 1998 bombing of bank offices in Rio Piedras and Santa Isabel, and the 1999 bombing of a highway in Hato Rey) remain under investigation. The radical separatist party, Los Macheteros, is involved of both of these attacks. Since 1999, the FBI has not reported terrorism in Puerto Rico.

Anarchists and radical socialist groups— many of whom, including the Workers' World Party, reclaim the streets and carnival against capitalism, have an international presence—sometimes often pose a possible challenge in the U.S. For example, anarchists, acting individually and in groups, caused most of the damage during the 1999 WTO ministerial meeting in Seattle. Special interest terrorism, the third type of domestic terrorism, differs from conventional right-wing and left-wing terrorism in that extremist special interest groups aim to address particular problems rather than affect systemic political reform. Extremists of special interest continue to commit acts of politically motivated violence to compel society members, including the general public, to alter views regarding topics deemed important to their causes. They dominate the radical fringes of animal rights, pro-life, climate, anti-nuclear, and other movements. Some special interest extremists — most prominently in animal rights and environmental movements — have gradually turned to vandalism and terrorist acts in attempts to advance their causes.

In recent years, the Animal Liberation Front —an extremist animal rights movement — has been one of America's most active radical components. Despite the negative aspects of ALF 's activities, its organizational policy discourages actions that harm "any animal, human and non-human." U.S. animal rights organizations, including ALF, usually adhered to this requirement. A distinct but related organization, the Earth Liberation Front

(ELF), assumed responsibility for the October 1998 arson fires at a ski resort in Vail (Colorado), which caused $12 million in damages. This incident is under investigation. Seven terrorist attacks in the U.S. during 2000 were linked to either ALF or ELF. Several additional actions committed during 2001 are being investigated for potential terrorist attacks.

International Terrorism

The U.S. faces a daunting foreign terrorist threat. The September 11 attack and USS Cole bombing in Aden, Yemen, in October 2000, as well as the prevention of Richard Reid 's apparent attempt to kill a Paris-to-Miami flight in December 2001, underline the spectrum of threats to U.S. interests raised by international terrorism.

Overall, the international terrorist threat to U.S. interests can be categorized into three categories: global international jihad movement, formalized terrorist groups, and international terrorism sponsors. Both of these categories affects U.S. interests abroad and in the U.S.

Today's most significant foreign terrorist threat to U.S. interests stems from Sunni Islamic extremists like Usama Bin Laden and his allies

Organization Al-Qaeda. The Taliban's militant Islamic regime harbored al-Qaeda leaders, including Usama Bin Laden, in Afghanistan since 1996. Despite recent military losses suffered by the Taliban and the apparent death of Al-Qaeda operational leader Mohamed Atef as a result of a U.S. bombing attack, Al-Qaeda must remain a strong and highly competent terrorist network. The network 's capacity and ability to inflict significant violence and devastation on U.S. persons and interests — as evidenced by the September 11 attack, the U.S. Cole bombing in October 2000, and the bombing of two U.S. embassies in East Africa in August 1998, among other plots — makes it a direct and immediate danger to the U.S.

However, Al-Qaeda 's threat is just part of the broader danger presented by the radical international jihad movement, consisting of individuals of different nationalities, ethnicities, sects, races, and memberships of militant groups working together to promote extremist Sunni goals. One of

Sunni extremists' primary objectives is to withdraw U.S. forces from the Persian Gulf region, most notably Saudi Arabia. The single common element among these diverse individuals is their adherence to the radical international jihad movement, which involves a radicalized philosophy and agenda advocating the use of violence against "Islamic enemies" to overthrow all non-Shariah (conservative Islamic) law governments. A primary operational goal of this movement was to plan and conduct large-scale, high-profile, high-casualty terrorist attacks against U.S. interests and civilians and their allies worldwide.

Richard Reid's

Richard C. Reid was arrested on December 22, 2001, after a flight attendant on American Airlines Flight 63 witnessed him trying to apparently ignite an improvised explosive in his sneakers on board the Paris-to-Miami flight. Passenger-assisted attendants overwhelmed and subdued Reid, and the flight was diverted to Boston, Massachusetts' Logan International Airport.

Evidence strongly indicates that Reid, traveling on a legitimate British passport, is associated with Al-Qaeda. Reid was convicted on nine charges, including putting an explosive device on an aircraft and attempted murder. Explosives in Reid's shoes, if exploded in some parts of the passenger cabin, may have blown a hole in the aircraft's fuselage.

Moussaoui Zacarias

The investigation also found that Reid and another perpetrator, Zacarias Moussaoui, were known associates. Moussaoui came to the FBI's notice, taking flight training classes in Minnesota in August 2001. Moussaoui paid over $8,000 in cash for flight simulator lessons on a 747-400 that much surpassed his pilot training. Moussaoui displayed a particular interest in the instructor's comment that aircraft doors can not be opened during flight. Moreover, his flight instructor was worried that Moussaoui was only interested in learning to take off and land the 747-400. In preparation for high-fidelity simulator training, he showed great interest in "piloting" a simulated flight from London Heathrow Airport to New York John F. Kennedy Airport. As the teacher took his questions to the FBI, the FBI and U.S.

Special Agents interrogated Moussaoui. Immigration and Naturalization (INS). He was found to be an INS overstay and detained by INS on August 16, 2001. Following his arrest, Moussaoui refused to allow his belongings to be searched, including a laptop computer and computer disk. Attempts were made to gain authority to search this machine. However, due to a lack of probable cause and lack of predication, no criminal or intelligence investigation could be done. Following the September 11 attack, a computer search was conducted. Nothing was found that linked Moussaoui to September 11 events; however, information on crop dusting was on the device. As a result, U.S. crop-dusting operations were suspended on two occasions in September 2001. On December 11, 2001, the U.S. District Court for Virginia's Eastern District indicted Moussaoui on six charges of conspiracy for his involvement on September 11, 2001.

The second foreign threat group is organized terrorist groups. These independent, transnational organizations have their own employees, infrastructure, financial arrangements, and training facilities. They may organize and launch foreign terrorist operations, and some actively promote U.S. terrorist-related activities. Extremist organizations such as Palestinian Hamas, the Irish Republican Army, Egyptian El-Gama Al-Islamiyya (I.G.), and Lebanese Hizballah have supporters in the United States, but the activities of these U.S.-based cells are mainly about fundraising, recruitment, and collecting low-level intelligence.

Hizballah is a formal organization with several anti-U.S. acts. Overseas attacks, including October 1983 U.S. car bombing. Lebanon's Naval Barracks. Except for Al-Qaeda, Hizballah is responsible for the deaths of more Americans than any other militant organization in the world. On June 21, 2001, the U.S. indicted 14 subjects—13 Saudis and 1 Lebanese national — for their alleged involvement in the June 1996 Khobar Towers bombing in Saudi Arabia. Nineteen U.S. airmen died in the blast; Saudi Hizballah is accused of attacking. To date, Hizballah has never launched a U.S. terrorist attack.

State terrorist sponsors are the third foreign threat group. The main supporters are Iran, Iraq, Sudan, and Libya. These countries see terrorism as a foreign-policy weapon. Syria, also on the U.S. Department of State's list of Foreign terrorist sponsors, has not been actively active in terrorist activity for many years, but also provides a safe haven for international terrorist organizations and loosely associated extremists. North Korea and Cuba — also on the State Department sponsor list — have greatly reduced their direct engagement with terrorism due in part to their economies' increasingly decreasing capacity to sustain such activity.

In perhaps the most notorious case of state-sponsored terrorism, Libya is suspected to be behind the December 1988 Pan Am Flight 103 bombing over Lockerbie, Scotland, which killed 270 people (259 on the plane and 11 on the ground). On April 5, 1999, the Libyan government handed over two former intelligence officers, Abd al-Basit al-Megrahi and Lamin Kalifah Fhima, to be tried for bombing by a special Scottish court in the Netherlands. Several years earlier, the FBI had put al-Megrahi and Fhima on its Top Ten Most Wanted Fugitives list, marking the first time that foreign government officials were identified. On January 31, 2001, Al-Megrahi was convicted of murder for his role in the bombing. Fhima was acquitted and released.

Of the seven nations identified as terrorist sponsors by the U.S., Iran represents the greatest threat to the U.S. Despite its anti-U.S. public neutrality. Since Mohammed Khatemi 's election in 1997, Iran's government, dominated by conservative clerics opposed to Khatemi, continues to harass critics and endorse anti-Western terrorism, both financially and logistically.

Weapons of Mass Destruction (WMD)

The trend toward high-profile, high-impact attacks comes at a time of increasing interest among domestic and foreign extremists in weapons of mass destruction (WMD). A series of anthrax-related incidents and threats since September 2001 offer an insight into evolving 21st-century terror scenarios.

Bioterrorism events using b. Anthracis spores sent by mail resulted in 22 anthrax cases and five deaths since October 3, 2001. Initial anthrax cases occurred in people with documented or suspected contact with open letters infected with b. Spores anthracis. Later, inquiries found four reported cases and one alleged case among postal workers who had no previous contact with open letters. This indicates that sealed envelopes infected with anthrax could be the cause of these exposures. The number of infected envelopes in the postal system is under investigation.

Leads are still investigated; however, no perpetrator was found. On November 9, 2001, the FBI released an offender's behavioral / linguistic evaluation focused on documented anthrax packages. As mentioned in this report, the suspect is assumed to be an adult male with access to anthrax source and the skills and experience to refine it. The FBI is heading a multi-agency campaign to locate such deadly attack perpetrators.

Since October 2001, the FBI has responded to over 8,000 use reports or threatened anthrax or other dangerous materials. Current anthrax threats outbreak marks a significant spike in a pattern of increased WMD cases that started in the mid-1990s. Over the past four years, there has been a relatively small number of incidents in the United States involving the use or threat of ricin. Before October 2001, there were no criminal cases involving actual use of anthrax in the U.S. To date, no evidence ties Al-Qaeda or any other terrorist group to these events.

Cyber / State Networks

Over the past few years, the FBI has identified a wide variety of cyber threats, ranging from website defacing by teenagers to sophisticated foreign-sponsored intrusions. Some of these events pose greater risks than others. Theft of national security information from a government entity or loss of electrical power to a major metropolitan area will have greater implications for national security, public security, and economy than website normal. But even the less extreme types have significant implications and can potentially undermine public trust in e-commerce and breach privacy or property rights. A website attack (or "hack") that closes an e-commerce site can have devastating consequences for a web-based company. An intrusion resulting in the theft of millions of credit card numbers from an online retailer will result in substantial financial losses and, more generally, decrease customer willingness to participate in e-commerce.

Beyond criminal threats, cyberspace also faces several major national security risks, including growing terrorist attacks.

Terrorist groups are rapidly using new I.T. and the Internet to formulate strategies, collect money, spread misinformation, and participate in encrypted communications. Cyberterrorism — meaning the use of cyber weapons to shut down vital national infrastructure (such as oil, transportation, or government operations) to coerce or threaten a government or civilian population — is an increasing danger.

On January 16, 2002, the FBI released a National Law Enforcement Telecommunications System warning on alleged terrorist efforts to use U.S. municipal and state websites to gain information on local energy networks, water reserves, dams, highly enriched uranium storage sites, and nuclear and gas facilities. While the FBI has no clear threat details about these apparent intrusions, terrorists pose significant challenges to our national security.

The FBI Response to Terrorism

The FBI built a robust response to domestic and foreign terrorist threats. Between fiscal years 1993 and 2003, the number of special agents committed to FBI counter-terrorism programs increased by around 224 percent (to 1,669—nearly 16 percent of all FBI special agents). In recent years, the FBI has improved its counter-terrorism policy to improve its ability to achieve these targets.

FBI Counterterrorism Center

As you know, Legislative funding helped enhance and extend the FBI's counter-terrorism capabilities. The FBI centralized several advanced organizational and analytical roles in the FBI Counter-Terrorism Center to strengthen its mission.

Established in 1996, the FBI Counter-terrorism Center battles terrorism on three fronts: international terrorism operations in both the U.S. and in support of extraterritorial investigations, domestic terrorism operations, and countermeasures related to foreign and domestic terrorism.

Eighteen federal agencies have a regular center presence and engage in their daily operations. These departments include, among others, Central Intelligence Agency,

Secret Service, and State Department. This multi-agency system offers an unparalleled opportunity for knowledge exchange, alert, and real-time analysis.

Cooperation interagency

This sense of collaboration has contributed to other big changes. Over the last few years, the FBI and CIA have established a closer working relationship, improving each agency's capacity to respond to terrorist threats and increasing the U.S. government's ability to respond to terrorist attacks.

An aspect of this partnership is ongoing staff exchange between the two agencies. A senior CIA case officer who serves as Deputy Section Chief for International Terrorism is included among CIA employees reported to the FBI Counterterrorism Division. FBI agents are also reported to the CIA, and a former special agent serves in a comparable role in the CIA counter-terrorist unit.

The National Infrastructure Hub

Created in 1998, the National Infrastructure Protection Center is an interagency center located at FBI headquarters that serves as a focal point for government efforts to alert and respond to domestic and foreign cyber intrusions. NIPC programs were developed in each FBI's 56 field offices.

FBI's Laboratory

The FBI Laboratory Division has developed a comprehensive response capability to support global counter-terrorism investigations. The FBI 's Mobile Crime Laboratory has the opportunity to gather and examine a variety of physical evidence on-scene. It has been used in major crime scenes like the bombing of the World Trade Center, Khobar Towers, and Eastern African Embassy bombings. The Mobile Crime Laboratory includes analytical instrumentation for rapid analysis and triage of explosives and other evidence obtained from crime scenes.

The Laboratory also enables the compact, self-contained Fly Away Laboratory (FAL) to react rapidly to criminal activities involving chemical or biological agents. The FAL consists of twelve suites of analytical instrumentation supported by a range of equipment enabling secure collection of hazardous materials, sample preparation, storage, and field setting analysis. The mobile crime laboratory and FAL 's key objectives are to enhance the protection of deployed personnel, generate leads through rapid review and screening, and conserve evidence for further investigation at the FBI Laboratory. The Laboratory has also formed agreements with many other federal agencies to rapidly and efficiently test chemical, biological and radiological materials. One collaboration, the Laboratory Response Network, is funded by the Centers for Disease Control and Prevention and Public Health Laboratories Association to evaluate biological agents.

Threat Warning

Since alert is key to preventing terrorist attacks, the FBI also extended the first terrorist threat warning system introduced in 1989. The system now covers all facets of law enforcement and intelligence. Currently, via this device, 60 federal agencies and their subcomponents receive information through secure teletype. Messages are also sent to all 56 FBI field offices and 44 Legats.

If threat information needs nationwide unclassified distribution to all federal, state, and local law enforcement agencies, the FBI sends messages through the National Telecommunications Enforcement System. Moreover, through the National Security Issues and Response (ANSIR) program, the FBI disseminates threat information to security managers of thousands of U.S. business interests around the globe. If warranted, the extended NTWS also helps the FBI to convey threat information directly to Americans.

On September 11, the FBI released a national threat alert via the National Threat Warning System, which is in effect until March 11, 2002, unless extended by the FBI. Since September 11, the FBI has disseminated 37 alerts through the NTWS. The FBI also provided over 40 lookout (BOLO) warnings through the NLETS system. BOLO alerts include FBI names of persons of investigative concern.

Via a 24-hour watch and other programs, the NIPC has established mechanisms to ensure all relevant outlets, including the U.S. intelligence community, FBI criminal investigations, other federal agencies, the private sector, and emerging intrusion detection technologies, and open sources, obtain relevant information in real-time or near-real-time. This knowledge is easily analyzed to decide whether a wide-scale attack is imminent or ongoing. Suppose a chemical, biological, nuclear or radiological substance is endangered. In that case, the FBI Mass Destruction Operations Unit (WMDOU) performs an interagency evaluation to determine the threat 's legitimacy, using subject matter experts and federal agencies with appropriate authority. Based on threat's credibility, WMDOU will coordinate federal assets' effective response. Based on this study, the FBI will issue alerts using various tools and disseminate alerts to relevant organizations in the U.S. government and the private sector so they can take immediate preventive measures.

The Future

I would finally like to speak briefly about measures we should take to further improve our ability to deter and investigate terrorist activity.

Encryption

One of these big measures includes the FBI 's encryption initiative. Communication is central to any collective effort — including criminal conspiracies. Like other suspects, terrorists are naturally hesitant to put their plot specifics on paper. They usually rely on oral or electronic communication to formulate their terrorist activity information.

Using commercially accessible, non-recoverable encryption devices by terrorist and other serious criminal activity individuals can effectively block access to this vital evidence by law enforcement. The failure of law enforcement to access encrypted messages and/or electronic data promptly severely impairs our ability to successfully detect and prosecute terrorist and/or other serious criminal actions.

This big threat to successful compliance presents substantial and extreme public safety implications. Unless the FBI strengthens its capacity to collect and analyze computer data collected through electronic surveillance, computer search and capture, and its ability to access the plain text of encrypted information, investigators and prosecutors will be denied timely access to useful information that could be used to deter and prosecute terrorist and other serious criminal actions.

Special Powers Joint Terrorism

Cooperation between law enforcement authorities at all levels is an essential component of the coordinated terrorist response. This partnership takes its most concrete operational form in the Joint Terrorism Task Forces approved in 44 nationwide cities. These task forces are especially well-suited to respond to terrorism because they combine the FBI's national and international investigative tools with local law enforcement officers' street-level experience. This cop-to-cop collaboration has been effective in stopping any possible terrorist attacks. Perhaps the most important cases came from New York City, where the City's Joint Terrorism Task Force was instrumental in thwarting two high-profile international terrorist plots — the series of bombings orchestrated by Shaykh Rahman in 1993 and the attempted subway bombing in New York City in 1997.

Not only were these attacks stopped, but today the conspirators who orchestrated them remain in federal jails thanks largely to the Joint Terrorism Task Force's extensive investigative work.

Since the end of 1999, following the Joint Terrorism Task Force model's popularity, the FBI has developed 15 new JTTFs. By the end of 2002, the FBI plans to develop or approve JTTFs in its 56 field divisions. By combining FBI investigative capabilities and local law enforcement agencies, these task forces are an important response to domestic and foreign terrorists' threats to U.S. communities.

Results

Improved analytical and organizational capabilities, along with enhanced collaboration and coordination, have improved the FBI's capacity to investigate and deter terrorist attacks.

In the past decade, hundreds of domestic extremists have been arrested and convicted. Among these are Timothy McVeigh, who in 1995 bombed the Murrah Federal Building in Oklahoma City. McVeigh was executed in June 2001 for perpetrating the worst domestic terrorism in the United States. More recently, on January 25, 2002, anti-abortion militant Clayton Lee Waagner was granted a total prison term of over 30 years for multiple charges of robbery and weapons, often accused of sending over 250 hoax anthrax letters to abortion clinics in October and November 2001.

Over the last ten years, the U.S. has charged over 60 topics connected with international terrorism. These include Ramzi Yousef, the organizational mastermind of the 1993 bombing of the World Trade Center and a plan to destroy U.S. airliners traveling far east (convicted in May 1997); Tsutomu Shirosaki, a Japanese Red Army member who shot rockets at the U.S. Embassy compound in Jakarta, Indonesia, 1986 (convicted in November 1997); and Gazi-Abu Mezer and Lafi Khalil, extremists who almost carried out a plot to attack the New York City subway system in 1997 (convicted in July 1998). From overseas since 1987, Yousef and Shirosaki were among the 16 fugitives prosecuted with terrorist-related activities. FBI / New York City Police Joint Terrorism Task Force narrowly averted the 1997 attempt to bomb the New York subway.

On October 18, 2001, four Al-Qaeda members received life sentences for their involvement in a plot to kill Americans resulting in East Africa's August 1998 embassy bombings. Mohamed Rashed Daoud al-Owhali, Khalfan Khamis Mohamed, Wadih el-Hage, and Mohamed Sadeek Odeh were convicted earlier in 2001 in New York's Southern District (SDNY) on several charges related to the bombing attempt. Two other subjects are facing trial in the SDNY.

Coordinated efforts by the FBI and other law enforcement/intelligence agencies were instrumental in reacting to the millennium threat revealed when Ahmed Ressam was caught trying to smuggle explosives across the U.S.-Canadian border near Seattle. After a trial in Los Angeles on April 6, 2001, Ressam was found guilty of all charges brought against him. Abdelghani Meskini, another suspect of involvement in the attempt to bomb Los Angeles airport, pled guilty in New York's Southern District on March 7, 2001, charges of providing material assistance to Ressam. On July 13, 2001, a third suspect, Mokhtar Haouari, was convicted of conspiracy charges. In January this year, Haouari was sentenced to 24 years in prison for his role in helping Ressam's attempt to carry out U.S. terrorist activity. One perpetrator, Abdelmajid Dahoumane, is in Algerian custody.

Moreover, several people have been arrested for participation in terrorist activity and are currently being investigated by the FBI. Usama Bin Laden and 15 other subjects are charged in Al-Qaeda and the U.S. Embassy bombings in East Africa in 1998. Three additional subjects are in detention in the United Kingdom but are due to be extradited in the SDNY shortly.

In October 2001, the FBI created the Most Wanted Terrorist initiative to concentrate on suspected terrorist suspects. Usama Bin Laden was among the first 22 names identified. In June 1998, Bin Laden was listed on the FBI's Top Ten Most Wanted Fugitives list.

US TERRORIST ATTACKS FAST FACTS

Notable fatal terror attacks on U.S. soil since 1980:

1978-1995-Three people die, and 23 others are injured during Ted Kaczynski 's mail bombings. "The Unabomber," as called, completes eight life terms for murder. He wasn't charged with terrorism, but the bombing series is considered a terror case.

February 26, 1993 — A bomb explodes on the second underground floor of Vista Hotel's public parking garage below New York 's 2 World Trade Center site. Six people are killed, and over 1,000 are treated for injuries. Six men are guilty of the attack. The seventh suspect, Abdul Rahman Yasin, remains broad.

April 19, 1995 — A bomb rips through the Federal Building in Oklahoma City, Oklahoma, killing 168 people and injuring nearly 700. Timothy McVeigh was convicted of federal murder in 1997 and executed in 2001.

July 27, 1996 — A bomb explodes in Atlanta's Centennial Olympic Park during the Summer Olympics. One person is killed, another dies from a heart attack, and over 100 others are wounded. Bombing suspect Eric Robert Rudolph was arrested in North Carolina in 2003 after being charged with Atlanta bombing and other bombings in 2000, including one at an abortion clinic where one person died. Rudolph serves four consecutive life terms, plus 120 years for the attacks.

September 11 2001 — Nineteen al-Qaeda members hijack four U.S. passenger airlines. Two are flown into New York's Twin Towers, one crashes into the Pentagon, and another crashes into the Pennsylvania countryside after passengers attempt to gain aircraft control to avoid an attack on the U.S. Capitol. 2.753 people are killed at World Trade Center site; 184 at the Pentagon; and 40 in Shanksville, Pennsylvania. Overall, 2,977 people are killed.

Chapter 10: HOW THE QANON CONSPIRACY THEORY WENT GLOBAL

Until recently, QAnon 's radical conspiracy theory was primarily an American phenomenon — a belief U.S. President Donald Trump secretly fights a "deep-state" cabal of pedophiles who control the world.

The far-right ideology has earned US followers as the presidential and congressional elections heat up in 2020. Trump has regularly retweeted messages from accounts endorsing QAnon, while over a dozen Republican candidates running for Congress endorsed some of its principles.

All this has raised fears about conspiracy-theory-driven domestic extremists listed by the FBI as a possible domestic terror threat. But QAnon no longer focuses solely on U.S. affairs.

According to QAnon researcher Marc-André Argentino, the unsubstantiated conspiracy hypothesis has gone global, fuelled by worldwide concern over the coronavirus pandemic.

"There's been tremendous growth," said Argentino, a Ph.D. candidate at Concordia University in Canada and a Global Extremism & Technology Network associate.

Conspiracy theories flourish in disasters, experts claim. With nervous citizens across the world seeking to make sense of the killer pandemic while leaders struggle to cope with it, at the end of a war called "The Storm," QAnon finds an eager audience with the hope of redemption from dictatorship.

According to Argentino, Germany, though spared the worst of the pandemic, is home to the largest number of QAnon followers overseas. One German QAnon channel on Telegram's encrypted messaging platform boasts 120,000 users.

Last month, the biggest increase in QAnon 's foreign followers came from Brazil, a pandemic hotspot where the virus killed over 100,000 citizens.

What does Q stand for?

"Q" is an anonymous person pretending to be a government insider with top-level security clearance and knowledge of the inner workings of the deep-state. The anonymous poster first appeared online in October 2017 when, with wild premonition, he went to the 4chan image board: former state secretary and Trump Democratic opponent Hillary Clinton would soon be arrested and riots will follow.

The prediction, needless to say, proved false, as did several others that followed, including other Democrats' mass indictment forecast. But that didn't stop Q from continuing to post about Trump's "hidden battle" against a deep pedophile state cartel, with his cryptic online "loss" parsed and amplified by a-faithful ecosystem.

A new conspiracy theory movement was born, with Q taking off where earlier "anons" like "FBIAnon" and "CIAAnon" petered out. What made QAnon stick was that it fell on Pizzagate 's heels, a 2016 conspiracy theory alleging the Democrats were running a child sex trafficking operation out of a pizza shop's basement.

That was never revealed. Although Q 's latest ramblings focus on deep-state efforts to undermine Trump's reelection, child violence and sex trafficking remain a constant part of his belief system.

In his last long-winded "fall" on July 31, Q ran that the coronavirus pandemic was partially intended to help "shelter" presumptive Democratic presidential nominee Joe Biden from appearing in public and engaging in debates, and to "eliminate" or postpone Trump rallies.

"At the heart of the present understanding of this philosophy, QAnon believes that President Trump is the person who can rescue the world from this network of bad actors and expose the deep state that exists in the United States and abroad," said Kevin Grisham, Associate Director of the Center for Hate and Extremism Studies at California State University in San Bernardino.

QAnon promoters say the deep state is all true, rejecting the notion of "worship" Trump or "Q."

"Qanon is a worldwide community of non-violent truthers / patriots committed to God, protecting our children from slavery and preventing Satanic DS (Deep State)," influential QAnon activist Joe Stroh, who recently tweeted "Obiwan Qenobi."

Who exactly is Q?

Despite wild speculation, no one unraveled Q's mystery individual. Outside QAnon circles, few consider him a true insider. Many analysts suspect over the years, more than one person might have been behind the Q account.

Who are QAnon adherents?

Although Q jumped from one imageboard to another, his followers thrived on mainstream platforms: Facebook, Twitter, YouTube and Telegram. According to Argentino, an estimated 300,000 to 400,000 people post about QAnon on Facebook, Twitter and Telegram every day, saying it would be a mistake to ignore them as "lunatics with tin foil hats living in their parents' basement."

Georgia businesswoman Marjorie Taylor Greene, who supports QAnon conspiracy theories, won a U.S. seat Republican primary election on Tuesday. Representative Assembly. She's expected to win seat in her heavily Republican congressional district in November.

Former National Security Advisor Michael Flynn appeared in a July 4 video reciting a famous QAnon slogan: "Where we go, we go all." Although Trump has not expressly supported the movement, he enjoys widespread support from QAnon supporters who attended his QAnon T-shirts rallies.

A Trump campaign spokeswoman has not addressed a question about whether Trump wants their support.

How has the pandemic impacted QAnon?

Since the coronavirus pandemic started, following QAnon has climbed rapidly. According to Argentino's study, the number of QAnon Facebook community members has jumped 800 percent to 1.7 million while Twitter accounts posting QAnon-related hashtags have risen 85 percent to 400,000.

In recent weeks, both Facebook and Twitter took down QAnon accounts for running out of their rules and guidelines. Further action is required.

But experts doubt the discipline would outlaw the campaign. For one, the conspiracy theory is speech-protected, and social media platforms can not literally mark QAnon as a "dangerous party." Second, banning QAnon followers from Facebook and Twitter will only deepen their belief in an information war against media insiders and those in the deep state, experts say.

"The crackdown just plays into their plot," Grisham said.

Romanian QAnon supporters take part in an anti-government rally to prevent the spread of COVID-19 infections, including wearing a face mask, in Bucharest, Romania, Aug. 10, 2020.

How popular is QAnon overseas?

The vast majority of QAnon's recent development has occurred overseas.

"You start seeing certain groups pop up everywhere," Grisham said.

Among countries with the biggest increases in QAnon activity: Germany, Britain, Australia, and Canada, followed by France, Italy, and New Zealand.

"The fact we see it distributed across the world indicates its importance to a global audience," Grisham said.

Although some QAnon followers see Trump as their savior, others believe local leaders will emerge to break their own deep states, Argentino said.

Chapter 11: HOW CONSPIRACY THEORIES ARE SHAPING THE 2020 ELECTION—AND SHAKING THE FOUNDATION OF AMERICAN DEMOCRACY

On her way to the post office, Jenny Mason is a busy mom: leather mini-backpack, brunet topknot, turquoise pedicure with matching ombré manicure. A Kenosha hairdresser, Wis., Jenny didn't vote in 2016 but has since been Donald Trump's big supporter. "Why the press dislike the president so much? "She 's telling. "I descended the rabbit hole. I started investigating a lot.

When I ask what research entails, something changes. Her voice has the same honey note, and her smile is as sweet as ever. But there's an eerie flash as she says, "This is where I don't know what I should tell because what's built into our system is steep. And it's about very corrupt, bad, dark stuff concealed from the public. Child sex trafficking is one.

Jenny might not even have known it, but she was parroting elements of QAnon's conspiracy theory, a pro-Trump viral paranoia that started in 2017 and has spread widely over recent months, spreading from far-right corners of the Internet to target ordinary citizens in the suburbs. His followers believe President Trump is a hero protecting the world from a "deep-state" cabal of Satan-worshiping pedophiles, Democratic politicians, and Hollywood celebrities running a global sex-trafficking ring, harvesting children's blood for life-sustaining chemicals.

That's not even remotely real. But an unprecedented number of Americans were exposed to crazy ideas. There are thousands and millions of QAnon groups and pages on Facebook, according to an internal company document checked by NBC News. Dozens of QAnon-friendly candidates ran for Congress, and at least three won GOP primaries. Trump called his followers "people loving our country."

In more than seven dozen interviews conducted in Wisconsin in early September, from the suburbs around Milwaukee to the scarred streets of Kenosha after the shooting of Jacob Blake, about 1 in 5 voters volunteered ideas into the field of conspiracy theory, ranging from QAnon to the suggestion that COVID-19 is a hoax. Two women in Ozaukee County calmly told me that an evil group maintains tunnels under the U.S. to rape, torture, and drink their blood. A supporter of Joe Biden near a Kenosha church told me votes don't matter, because "elites" will determine the election outcome anyway. A woman on a street corner in Kenosha clarified that Democrats are trying to put in U.N. Pre-election troops to avoid Trump's victory.

It's hard to know why people believe what they believe. Some were revealed online to QAnon conspiracy theorists. Others appeared to echo false theories in Plandemic, a pair of conspiracy videos featuring a debunked former viral medical researcher, spreading the suggestion that COVID-19 is a hoax through social media. When asked where they found their results, almost all these voters were cryptic: "Go online," one woman said. "Dig deep," another said. They seemed to share the corporate media 's mutual disdain — a cynicism that has only grown greater and deeper since 2016. The truth wasn't mentioned, they said, and that wasn't true.

Not just because of what these voters believe, but also because they don't. The facts that should underpin a sense of common truth are irrelevant for them; news reports that should usually persuade their vote fall on deaf ears. They won't be swayed by statistics on coronavirus deaths, they won't be convinced by job losses or stock market gains, and they won't care if Trump, as the Atlantic claimed, called America's fallen soldiers "losers" or "suckers," because they won't believe it. Messaging, ads, or data are impervious. Not only infected with conspiracy; they seem to be inoculated against fact.

Democracy depends on an educated, active public to respond rationally to the real-life facts and challenges before us. But that untethered an increasing number of Americans. "They 're not on the same epistemological basis, they 're not working in the same worlds," says Whitney Phillips, Syracuse professor researching online misinformation. "You can't have a working democracy until people at least share the same solar system."

American politics was often susceptible to paranoia. Historian Richard Hofstadter famously called it "an arena for angry minds." In the late 18th and early 19th centuries, Americans were persuaded that the Masons were an anti-government conspiracy; populists in the 1890s warned of "hidden cabals" manipulating the gold price; McCarthyism and the John Birch Society sparked a wave of anti-communist paranoia in the 20th century that infected t Recently, Trump helped sow a racist myth that Barack Obama wasn't born in the U.S.

As a candidate in 2016, every week Trump seemed to endorse a new crazy plot, from tying Ted Cruz 's father to Kennedy's assassination to proposing the murder of Supreme Court Justice Antonin Scalia. That year, in interviews at Trump rallies, I heard voters support all kinds of delusions: that the government was run by drug cartels; that Obama was a third term foreign-born Muslim; that Hillary Clinton assassinated Vince Foster. But after four years of Trump presidency, paranoia is no longer limited to society's margins. According to Pew Research Center, 25 % of Americans suggest there is some merit to the conspiracy theory that the COVID-19 pandemic was orchestrated deliberately. (Virologists, global health officials and U.S. national-security officials all discounted the suggestion that the pandemic was man-made, while Trump administration officials said they could not rule out the possibility that it was the result of a laboratory accident.) In a new poll of nearly 1,400 left-leaning Civiqs / Daily Kos, more than half of the Republican population.

I heard false conspiracies from average Americans over a week of interviews in parking lots and boutiques and strip malls from Racine to Cedarburg to Wauwatosa, Wis. Shaletha Mayfield, Racine's Biden supporter, says she thinks Trump developed COVID-19 and will bring it back in the fall. Courtney Bjorn, who voted for Clinton in 2016 and plans to vote for Biden, lowered her voice as she speculated about the powers behind the devastation in her neighborhood. "No rich people lost homes," she says. "What profits when communities burn? But the biggest illusions I encountered came from the right voters.

About one-third of the Trump supporters I talked with some sort of conspiratorial thought. "COVID may have been published by communist China to bring down our economy," says John Poulos, loading grocery stores outside Sendik's grocery store in Wauwatosa's Milwaukee suburb.

"COVID was made," says Maureen Bloedorn, stepping into Kenosha's Dollar Tree. She didn't vote for Trump in 2016, but expects to help him in November, partially because "he gave Obama a bill for all his holidays that he took on the American dime." This concept was popularized by a fake news article that appeared on a satirical website and went viral. Marcella Frank and Tina Arthur and told me they intend to vote for Trump again on a cigarette break outside their small business in Ozaukee County because they are profoundly disturbed by "the cartel." They received "numerous rumors" that the COVID-19 tents set up in New York and California were supposedly for children rescued from underground sex-trafficking tunnels.

Arthur and Frank clarified they 're not QAnon followers.

Frank says she spends much of her free time investigating child sex trafficking, although Arthur adds she also finds this information on Yandex, a Russian-owned search engine. Frank 's eyes fill with tears as she explains what she's found: children being raped and tortured so that "the cartel" can "extract and drink their blood." She claims Trump confiscated the blood on the black market as part of his battle against the cartel. "I think if Biden wins, the world's over," Arthur says. "Honestly, I 'd try to leave country. And if that wasn't a choice, I 'd probably take my kids, sit in the driveway, turn my car on and it'd be done. The increase of conspiratorial thought is the result of many interrelated trends: decreasing institutional trust; the decline of local news; a social media climate that makes gossip easy to propagate and difficult to debunk; a president who sticks to whatever and everyone he feels can help his political fortunes.

It's all part of our cabling. "The brain likes mad," says Nicco Mele, Harvard 's former Shorenstein Center director, who studies the spread of online misinformation and conspiracies. Therefore, experts claim, algorithms on websites like Facebook and YouTube are built to deliver content that confirms existing beliefs – learning what users are searching for and feeding them more and more provocative content in an effort to keep them on their pages. All this stupidity leads to a political imbalance.

On the right, conspiracy theories make Trump's supporters even more loyal to the president, who many see in the "deep state" as a fighter against enemies. It also protects him from an October surprise, as no matter what news about Trump, a growing U.S. electorate simply won't believe it. On the left, however, conspiracy theories also undermine Biden's allegiance by making people less likely to trust the voting process. If they conclude that their votes won't matter when mysterious leaders pull the country's strings, why bother going through the trouble of casting a ballot? Experts studying misinformation claim nothing will change before Facebook and YouTube move their business model away from conspiracy-rewarding algorithms.

"Nowhere near peak we 're nuts," says Mele. Phillips, Syracuse professor, admits that things get weirder. "We 're troubled," she says. "Words don't describe what a nightmare scenario is." But to voters like Jenny Mason, it seems more like a mass awakening.

Trump "reveals these things," she says serenely, with her turquoise-tipped fingernails. "Americans' eyes are opened to the darkness once concealed." After morning yoga, Jenny says, she also spends hours watching videos, immersing herself in a world she believes to bring her closer to the reality.

"You can't resist because it's too addicting to know what kind of world we 're living in," she says. "We live in alternate reality."

Chapter 12: HOW COVID-19 MYTHS ARE MERGING WITH THE QANON CONSPIRACY THEORY

At first glance, all they seem to have in common is their vast distance from reality.

On the one hand, QAnon: a complex conspiracy theory that claims that President Trump is waging a covert war against Satan-worshiping bourgeois paedophiles.

On the other side, a swirling cloud of pseudoscience alleging coronavirus doesn't exist, or isn't lethal, or any number of other groundless arguments.

These two theories are coming together in a grand conspiracy mash-up.

Related.

It emerged on London streets last weekend, where speakers addressing thousands of followers at an anti-mask, anti-lockdown protest touched on both themes. Posters supporting QAnon and other conspiracy theories were on view.

Sunday, President Trump retweeted a post saying the real number of Covid-19 deaths in the U.S. was a small fraction of official figures. Twitter later removed the tweet under its misinformation guidelines.

The user that posted it-" Mel Q-is still "alive, a copious spreader of QAnon 's ideas.

QAnon's key theme is that President Trump is leading a battle against sex trafficking that ends in a day of reckoning with the detention and execution of influential politicians and journalists.

Mel Q is only one of the QAnon influencers plugging coronavirus misinformation.

The merger of QAnon and Covid-19 conspiracies is also visible in a number of BBC documents.

"Coronavirus is a cover-up for... child sex trafficking-a big problem in this world and nobody wants to investigate," read one typical email.

Another man got in contact to explain how his mother — who joined the protests — was led down the rabbit hole over the course of the pandemic, first taken by the coronavirus conspiracy theories, and now by QAnon.

Pedophiles, anti-vaxxers, 5 G

QAnon influencers and pandemic conspiracies have long overlapped, but weekend demonstrations in London and other cities around the world were the largest offline demonstration of their the links to date.

"Covid theory theorists find ready-made targets in the QAnon crowd and vice versa," says Chloe Colliver, senior policy analyst at the Institute for Strategic Dialog (ISD), a think-tank focusing on extremism.

"Faced with the pandemic, conspiracy theories picture a world organized and controllable," explains Jovan Byford, psychologist at Open University. "Conspiracy theories thrive when social structure breaks down, and attempts to make sense of the world prove insufficient for what is happening."

Although the pandemic has increased the overall potential audience for such concepts, the QAnon and coronavirus strands are also connected by a concern — or obsession — with children and their welfare.

That's why we've seen these ideas spread in local Facebook groups, where more innocent discussions cover which cafes are baby-friendly or which local schools are graduating.

"Child abuse is the epitome of moral and sexual depravity and something unquestionably bad," says Jovan Byford, "so its integration into the theory helps push the concept of the conspirators' monstrosity and iniquity to the full, unquestionable maximum."

Conspiracy stream

Some of those in Saturday's crowd were likely attracted by legitimate concerns about mental health, environment, government policy criticism, or questions about still-evolving research.

But, mostly, what attendees learned from the speakers was a constant stream of bad information (about coronavirus death rates), groundless speculation (about child violence and "mandatory" vaccinations) and unfounded allegations (about the pandemic being orchestrated by governments or mysterious powers-or, in the words of the conspiracy theorists, a "plandemic").

"The vast majority of the material was about conspiracies," says Joe Mulhall, a senior Hope Not Hate researcher, an advocacy organization that monitors far-right and conspiracy movements.

"Very little came from a positive point of view. No speakers spoke about, for example, the effect of the lockout on small businesses," says Mulhall, who was at Saturday's gathering.

And the UK was not limited to conspiratorial thought-similar signs could be seen in weekend protests in Boston, Berlin, and elsewhere. QAnon and conspiracy theories of coronavirus have really gone worldwide.

Spreading fast

"What concerns us is that these lines of thought are connected to a super-conspiracy with QAnon as its foundation," says Hope Not Hate's Joe Mulhall. "Q helps you to connect the dots with all the various conspiracies – there's a hidden conspiracy behind the scenes doing stuff. And as soon as you speak about super-conspiracies and hidden hands, it's a quick step to the 'other' and, in many instances, it's 'Jews.'

"Anti-Semitism is never far from these conspiracy theories," he says.

"Potential audiences for dangerous disinformation are growing and harder to isolate and contain," says ISD's Chloe Colliver. "They're becoming so interconnected that it's hard for tech platforms at this late stage to grip on limiting the reach of potentially dangerous disinformation now."

In recent weeks, Twitter has acted to remove a number of large QAnon accounts; Facebook has closed a large number of QAnon groups; and thousands of QAnon Instagram pages have been deleted.

In response, the conspiracy theorists switched to new slogans and hashtags — for example, # SaveTheChildren.

The rising conspiracy movement, though still on the fringes, seems to pick up steam on the streets.

"We can't pick up all the activities together," says Joe Mulhall. "They 're setting up so quickly."

THE ALLEGATIONS AGAINST QAnon

Why is it so important?

There's no question that the charges are devastating and harmful. But there are plenty of malicious and dangerous allegations floating around the internet, many of which go unnoticed.

For a few important reasons, QAnon is more dangerous: the very misleading accusations it makes are being transmitted to many people, many of whom do not know that they are fak. It bears many parallels to Pizzagate, which ended in real violence when a person entered a pizza restaurant with a weapon.

An FBI intelligence newsletter last year indicated that followers could pose a threat to domestic terrorism. Although certain acts of violence allegedly influenced by QAnon have been taking place, for the time being, they were mainly minor and committed by what appears to be a small minority of adherents of the theory.

In July, Twitter said it would stop promoting QAnon content and accounts in a move that it predicted would affect some 150,000 accounts. It said it would block QAnon URLs and permanently suspend QAnon accounts, which organize harassment or violate its rules.

In August, Facebook suspended nearly 800 QAnon groups for posts that promoted abuse, displayed intent to use weapons, or attracted followers with trends of violent behavior. It has also placed limitations on the remaining 1,950 QAnon public and private groups identified by it. Facebook said it plans to prohibit advertising supporting or mentioning QAnon, and it does not allow QAnon pages to operate business stores.

A spokeswoman for TikTok's short-form video app said QAnon content "frequently includes misinformation and hate speech" and removed hundreds of hashtags from QAnon.

A Reddit spokeswoman told Reuters that since 2018 when she took down forums such as r / great awakening, the site has deleted QAnon communities, which have repeatedly violated its rules.

A spokesperson for YouTube said she has deleted tens of thousands of Q-related videos and terminated hundreds of Q-related channels for breaching her rules after updating her policy on hate speech in June 2019.

YouTube also said it is that its recommendations for some QAnon videos that "could misinform users in negative ways." It has no clear ban on monetizing QAnon material. ISD researchers found that about 20% of all Facebook posts related to QAnon featured ties to YouTube.

Reviews on major Amazon.com Inc and Etsy Inc e-commerce sites show retailers selling QAnon-branded products ranging from books to T-shirts and face masks.

The senior pastor of Round Grove Baptist Church in Miller, Missouri, Mark Fugitt, recently sat down to count the conspiracy theories people in his church post on Facebook. The list had been a long one. It included reports that 5 G radio waves are being used to manipulate the mind. That the murder of George Floyd is a hoax; that Bill Gates is connected to the devil; that masks can destroy you; that the theory of germs is not real; and that after all there may be anything to Pizzagate.

"You just don't see this often," Fugitt said. "If it is ever released, you can see it five to ten times. That's sure to escalate."

Theories of conspiracy.

Great theories aimed at showing that influential forces are secretly manipulating events and structures for sinister purposes — are nothing new in the U.S. But a sort of ur-conspiracy theory, QAnon, has merged in online forums since 2017 and has produced millions of believers. "Seeing QAnon is seeing not only a conspiracy theory but the emergence of a new religion," Adrienne LaFrance wrote in June in The Atlantic.

Named after "Q," who anonymously posts 4chan on the online message board, QAnon says that President Donald Trump and military officials are trying to uncover a pedophile "deep-state" network with ties to Hollywood, the media, and the Democratic Party. The theory has attracted adherents since its first mention some three years ago, in search of a straightforward way to describe recent disorienting global events.

QAnon is no longer radical, but the obsession of far-right activists and their supporters. It has gained popularity both on the web and in the offline world with the help of Trump and other elected officials. In Georgia, a candidate for Congress has hailed Q as a "mythical hero," and at least five other Congressional hopefuls from Illinois to Oregon have expressed their support.

One scholar found an increase of 71 percent in QAnon content on Twitter and an increase of 651 percent on Facebook since March.

Jon Thorngate is the pastor of LifeBridge, a non-denominational congregation of about 300 in a suburb of Milwaukee. His members have posted "Pandemic" on Facebook in recent months, he said, a half-hour film that portrays COVID-19 as a money-making scheme by government officials and others. Members also went around a now-banned Breitbart video, which promotes hydroxychloroquine as a virus remedy.

Thorngate, one of the few pastors who would go on record among those who found QAnon a real issue in their churches, said the videos are usually posted online by just five to 10 members. But he's found in discussions with other members that many more are prone to conspiracy theories than the ones commenting.

Thorngate partially attributes the phenomenon to the "death of expertise"—a mistrust of figures of authority that causes some Americans to undervalue long-established competency and knowledge steps. Among some members of the church, he said, the mentality is, "I will use the church for the things I like, disregard it for the things I don't like, and find my reality.

"That part is troubling for us because nothing now feels authoritative."

For years in the 1980s and 1990s, U.S. evangelicals, above almost any other group, cautioned of what would happen when people abandon absolute truth. (which they are found in the Bible), suggesting that the concept of partial reality will lead people to believe in something that reinforces their inner hunches. But big government skepticism, challenging scientific orthodoxy (on evolution, for instance) and denying Hollywood values and liberal elites took root among millennial Christians, many of whom felt politically marginalized and beaten up

by mass media. For QAnon, they're normal
targets.

CONCLUSION

QAnon is the umbrella word for a wide variety of internet conspiracy theories that wrongly say the world is run by a group of Satan-worshiping pedophiles who plot against Mr. Trump while running a global child sex-trafficking network.

To be sure, QAnon remains a "popular-opinion fringe phenomenon," since research shows that "most people do not know what it is, let alone believe it," Dartmouth professor Nyhan said.

"But if their revealed philosophy encourages them to commit aggression, that is potentially dangerous," he said. "I am also concerned about the way believers in 'Q' have become more prominent and powerful online and inside the base of the Republican Party."

QAnon followers claim this clique includes top Democrats including Hillary Clinton, Barack Obama, and George Soros, as well as a variety of entertainers and celebrities from Hollywood such as Oprah Winfrey, Tom Hanks, Ellen DeGeneres, and religious figures including Pope Francis and the Dalai

Lama. Many of them even claim that, besides molesting children, members of this group kill and eat their victims to extract a life-extending chemicals from their blood.

Mr. Trump was persuaded by top military officers to run for president in 2016 to crack this criminal enterprise, end his domination over politics and media, and bring his members to justice.

The QAnon phenomenon seems to develop with unprecedented speed and dexterity across America's social media landscape in recent months, with a 71% rise in Twitter content and a 651% rise in Facebook pages and groups since March, according to researcher Marc-André Argentino, a PhD candidate at Concordia University in Montreal, Canada, who studies the connection between technology.

Although mysterious internet groups have grown expert at sidestepping platform restrictions by adopting new identities and hashtags, researchers can still track recognizable QAnon-affiliated content, as much of it has been limited only recently. According to Argentino 's study, QAnon — which imagines Trump operating in secret against a global conspiracy of pedophiles —

expanded from its inception in 2017 to March 2020 to more than 220,000 members of QAnon-related Facebook groups. It's swelled to at least 1.7 million members since March.

In recent years, people who believe in QAnon conspiracies have also been involved with a variety of strange real-life events, including a man using a blind truck to block traffic on the Hoover Dam in 2018. When authorities arrived, the man stood by his car with a sign unfurled to show a famous QAnon rallying cry.

According to the Associated Press, the man wrote a letter ending with the expression "Where we go one, we go all," a term widely used on QAnon forums and conspiracy theory websites.

A man accused of fatally shooting suspected Gambino mafia boss Francesco "Franky Boy" Cali last year claimed Cali was part of the "deep state," court records said.

In court records, Anthony Commello's defense attorney said his client, based on interviews with the accused shooter's relatives, "became more outspoken about his support for QAnon," about six weeks before Cali 's murder. "However [his] support for QAnon went beyond mere involvement in a radical political group, it grew into a psychotic obsession... He ardently believed that [Cali] was a popular deep-state member and, therefore, a suitable target for citizen arrest."

CPSIA information can be obtained
at www.ICGtesting.com
Printed in the USA
LVHW051110060221
678444LV00003B/248